"Interesting and readable — I completed it in one evening! It is a good guide for anyone who wants to excel and be successful in the service industry."

Abdullah Mat Zaid, Malaysia Airlines

"Self-empowerment, measurable goals, practical skills; John Tschohl tells how service providers can become HeroZ!"

William C. Byham, Ph.D., Author
Zapp! The Lightening of Empowerment

"The YMCA is in the people-serving business. John Tschohl's new book continues the challenge for every one of our employees to be the #1 professional in our organization. Another great contribution for service training!"

Len Wilson, National Field Executive, YMCA

"John Tschohl has done it again! If you are a service provider, *CA\$HING IN* will help you rise up and cash in through service to others! Tschohl, the *Customer Service Guru*, outlines the steps of self improvement, service improvement, and qualities necessary to succeed by serving. In today's environment of the masses crying for service, *CA\$HING IN* is a must read."

Dr. Lyman K. Steil, CSP, CPAE
Communication Development

"People that think and perform with the thoughts John Tschohl provides in this book are going to be the winners of tomorrow."

C.P. Luis Felipe Salas Benavides, Direccion General
Benavides, Mexico

"An outstanding road map for taking charge of your destiny and achieving success in the growing service industry."
Roger Dow, Vice President, Marriott Hotels/Resorts/Suites

"John Tschohl has hit another service home run. *CA$HING IN* is for every service professional who wants to create raving fan customers. The book beautifully integrates self improvement thinking with key service concepts. Read it!"
Ken Blanchard, Co-author, The One Minute Manager

"*CA$HING IN: Make More Money, Get A Promotion, Love Your Job* delivers even more than the title promises. John Tschohl's book provides excellent results-oriented information. If you want to make fast progress in your career, *CA$HING IN* is must reading!"
Paul J. Meyer, Founder, Success Motivation Institute, Inc., Leadership Management, Inc., Meyer Family Enterprises

"John Tschohl's insight into the area of customer service is truly remarkable. His concepts apply well in any type of customer oriented business."
Christopher T. Murdock, Star Enterprise/Texaco

"Tschohl's visualization and affirmation techniques are the keys to success in both service and your personal life! Follow these tips and you will get the raise you've been waiting for! *CA$HING IN* is a must read!"
Vince Lombardi, Jr.

"This book is a practical hands on guide for service providers to focus their energy on getting what they want and the steps to get there."

> *Lisa Ford, Author*
> How to Give Exceptional Customer Service

"There is not an employee in the United States who would not benefit from CA$HING IN. Full of nuggets."

> *Bill Irwin, Vice President of Operations*
> *American Logistics Association*

"John Tschohl reaches out to every service provider to encourage tapping into their power to choose to provide quality service and become self-motivated to develop success plans leading to career accomplishment and recognition."

> *Lee Noel, Senior Executive and Chairman of the Board*
> *Noel-Levitz Centers*

"John Tschohl got it! He'll show you how to get the attitude, visualize and then CA$H IN."

> *Stuart Philstrom, Bloomington Speedy Car Wash*

"CA$HING IN is a practical guide to reaching success in professional and personal activities. John Tschohl approaches many essential aspects of a successful journey — efficient use of time, empowerment, win-win practice, positive posture and optimism."

> *Sergio Cezar de Azevedo, Quality Manger*
> *Golden Cross, Brazil*

"What an interesting book! Thirty chapters packed with valuable information, presented simply, clearly, and powerfully. This is a great book for any person who wants to grow personally and professionally."

Nido R. Qubein, Chairman, Creative Services, Inc.

"*CA$HING IN* is a self-study learning module offering an excellent training tool to facilitate any persons self-assessment of his/her attitude, behavior, and self-directness toward achieving success in customer relations."

Herb Stokes, Director of Quality Management
Allied Van Lines, Inc.

"Businesses throughout the world have much to gain by reading *CA$HING IN*. Tschohl has truly elevated customer service to a highly refined form of art."

Alvaro Castro-Harrigan, Universidad Latinoamericana

"John Tschohl has been showing business people how to be happier with their jobs and serve their customers better for as long as I've known him. He is an avid student of what makes businesses successful and he shares this wisdom in his new book, *CA$HING IN*. I recommend you read it and pay close attention. There's value here."

Jim Cathcart, Author, Relationship Selling

"After reading *CA$HING IN*, I felt strongly motivated to share it with all the providers in my medical group. I started to introduce my group into this new experience and we are all very satisfied with the results obtained so far."

Ignacio Aguilar Girbau, Servicios Medicos AGYA S.A., Mexico

"With a descriptive, inspiring blueprint, *CA$HING IN* movingly and clearly instructs us how to believe in ourselves, visualize success, capitalize on opportunities for promotion, become an enthusiastic member of any team and establish well-defined objectives and standards to achieve healthy and gratifying goals."

Jim Ramstad, Member of Congress

"This pro-active approach is the leading edge in career guidance to help you visualize and realize your goals by paving your own road to a more confident, focused and happier you."

Jack Murphy, Chief Operating Officer
PHP Healthcare Corporation

"Tschohl provides a handy source of easily referenced tools and skills to help service providers at all levels continuously improve their performance and potential. This book is a great working guide for getting better business results through more responsive, win-win relationships with internal and external customers."

Anthony R. Montebello, Ph.D., Author
Work Teams That Work

"*CA$HING IN* — A practical approach to individual growth and organizational improvement."

Marlan Carlson, Manager
3M Quality Management Services

"Simply delightful reading — one of the most enlightening and motivational books available today."

Daniel M. Ochy, Marketing Manager
GBM de Panama S.A.

CA$HING IN

*Make More Money,
Get A Promotion,
Love Your Job*

JOHN TSCHOHL

Publisher's Cataloging in Publication

Tschohl, John
    Cashing in: make more money, get a promotion, love your job / by John Tschohl.
    p. cm.
    Includes bibliographical references.
    ISBN 0-9636268-2-5

    1. Customer service   I. Title

HF5415.5.C44 1995
658.8'12'0285—dc20   94-74532
                                                       CIP

Table of Contents

Acknowledgments   v
About the Author   vii
Foreword   ix
Service Professionals: This Book Is For You   xi
Preface   xv

Section I: Self Improvement   1
1   Self Development   3
2   Importance of Personal Development   7
3   Self Concept   17
4   How to be Successful   29
5   Attitude Determines Action   33
6   Be Pro-Active   41
7   Self Image   45
8   Desire   51
9   How to be Your Own Teacher   55
10 The Win-Win Paradigm   59
11 Pursue Self Improvement Aggressively   65
12 How to Get Noticed   71

Section II: Service Improvement   77
13 Self Image   81
14 Being A Good Listener   87
15 Handling Complaints   95
16 It's Not What You Say But How You Say It   101
17 Consider Yourself Empowered   105
18 Relationships Are Vital   109
19 Doing More Than Necessary   113
20 Each Customer: An Individual   117
21 Quality   121

Section III: Qualities of Successful People   123
22 Joy In Your Work   125
23 Humor's Benefits   129
24 How to Learn A Sense of Humor   133
25 Empower Yourself   137
26 Time   147
27 Service Recovery   151
28 Energize   157
29 Leisure   161
30 Weekend Neurosis   165

Conclusion: A Winner Never Quits   169
Management: Support Employee Education   175
Solution to Nine Dot Exercise   183
Resources   185

Acknowledgments

No author has ever written a book without help and I am no exception.

Hazel Brown has been my strong right arm for 21 years and has generously provided me with support throughout the development of this book. She is a true service professional and an excellent model for all service providers. Others know her as the Vice President of Administration for Service Quality Institute.

The staff at Service Quality Institute extended their patience and encouragement once again as I took on yet another book. Without each one of them, this book would not have come about.

Steve Franzmeier has helped me through the writing process of all three of my books. I have worked with him for over eight years and he continues to generate new and exciting ideas for my books.

Best Sellers Publishing, headed by Shannon Kranz, not only published the book, but also took part in its creation. They challenged my every word and pushed me to write the best book I could.

My wife, Pat, and my two children, Matthew and Christina, also deserve a great amount of thanks. They willingly endure not only my passion for customer service, but also our many vacations filled with publicity interviews and book signings.

My mother, Agnes Tschohl, age 94, is more responsible for my success than anyone. My father died when I was seven years old, and she raised me and developed in me a strong self concept and belief in myself.

About the Author

John Tschohl is founder and president of Service Quality Institute, a multi-national firm specializing in quality service. His company developed the world's first comprehensive customer service training system.

The author of numerous articles and publications on customer service, Tschohl has developed and authored over 45 books and learning systems. His technology is used by organizations throughout the world to improve their levels of customer satisfaction.

Tschohl is an internationally-recognized speaker and trainer and has consulted with some of America's top companies. Tschohl is an active member of National Speakers Association and Instructional Systems Association.

Tschohl's international clients include companies in Mexico, South Africa, Brazil, Canada, Israel, Malaysia, and Singapore. His technology has been culturally adapted and translated into a number of foreign languages.

Tschohl's first book, *Achieving Excellence Through Customer Service* (Prentice Hall, 1991), provides managers with practical steps to implement and manage a quality service strategy.

In his second book, *The Customer Is Boss: A Practical Guide For Getting What You Paid For And More* (Best Sellers Publishing, 1993), Tschohl teaches consumers how to effectively challenge bad customer service and gain satisfaction in dealing with service providers.

Foreword

As America seeks to improve its global competitiveness in the increasingly important international and domestic markets, it is paramount our nation encourage individuals to pursue self-empowerment in their daily lives.

CA$HING IN shows us the way!

We can't look to the government to solve our competitive disadvantages in the marketplace.

Our country's people must embark on an exciting and profitable journey of self-development that will lead to better customer service, polished personal skills, enhanced value to employers and heightened self-confidence. That's the American way!

Improved customer service, in the broadest possible sense, is something every American must seek with renewed vigor. There are grave consequences for our nation's economy if we do not step forward to take on the world.

With a descriptive, inspiring blueprint, CA$HING IN movingly and clearly instructs us how to believe in ourselves, visualize success, capitalize on opportunities for promotion, become an enthusiastic member of any team and establish well-defined objectives and standards to achieve healthy and gratifying goals.

As Minnesota's only member of the U.S. House Small Business Committee, I've talked with thousands of employees and visited hundreds of businesses. CA$HING IN could help them all. The future is in our hands!

While that may seem like common sense, CA$HING IN demonstrates how far too often the lack of self-respect translates into poor customer service. You forcefully and persuasively prove that self-confidence, achieved through a well delineated set of objectives and self-affirmation, leads to an attitude where we can "expect success." And as Tschohl so succinctly states: "Self confidence is power."

The power and effectiveness of CA$HING IN resides in the step-by-step outline it lays out that anyone can implement in their daily professional life. "You are responsible," is the underlying, freedom-generating message. I only wish I could get all 435 members of the U.S. House to read this great book and take it to heart.

Tschohl is a truly effective teacher. In CA$HING IN, he teaches the reader how to solve problems, inspire ourselves, become members of the team, find humor in our work and, perhaps most critical of all, to remember that "quality service is whatever customers think it is."

> *— Jim Ramstad*
> *Member of Congress*

Service Professionals: This Book Is For You

Let's say that you work in a service business. You're a salesperson or an office worker. You have a family...or you plan to have one. Maybe you need to improve your standard of living. The real money in your company seems out of reach. You have little hope for promotion. You never get any quality service training, so you aren't improving your qualifications. You're thinking about getting another job.

I have a suggestion: Develop your skills *yourself!* You can do it. It doesn't take a lot of money, just time and determination.

Your success is much too important to be left to the decisions of others.

When I went into the personal development business in 1970, I found myself totally dependent upon my own skills. Soon I realized that the only way that I could survive was to teach myself how to sell. I read every book on selling and listened to every audio cassette on selling and closing skills that I could find. My sales increased substantially. After a couple years I realized that I knew more about selling than 99 percent of the salespeople in the world. So, I also started to teach professional selling.

You, too, can read books, listen to audio cassettes, and view video cassettes. If you have a home computer, obtain software (including CD-ROM discs) that contains information on customer service and self-development.

The trouble with many service businesses is that they try to shortcut the road to quality customer service. Executives think that if they say "We have customer-friendly service in this company" the good genie will make it so. They overlook the fact that quality customer service, like most things in life, can be obtained only with hard work.

This situation isn't likely to change soon, so your future is up to *you*. You've got to take the bull by the horns, as the rodeo clown does. What should you do? I suggest:

Compare yourself with yourself instead of with others.

(1) Believe in yourself. To measure your progress, compare yourself with *yourself*, instead of with others. Abolish self-imposed limitations and see yourself as you *want* to be, not as you are today.

(2) Visualize yourself in your boss's job or in *his* boss's job. In your mind's eye see yourself acting and feeling like a person making more money in the important job that you set your eyes on.

(3) Write a personal *Mission Statement* that consists of objectives and standards.

• Objective: To deliver exceptional service every day.

• Standard: Smile and show I care with every customer.

(4) List specific steps to improve *your own* circumstances in life. Become pro-active.

Become pro-active.

- Learn the contents of your company's Quality Service Standards. Re-read the Standards once a month.

- Do *more* and learn *more* than customers and your boss expect. Become valuable to your company.

Preface

Training service workers in the strategies and tactics of service is not customary. What *is* customary is the training of managers to *supervise* service workers.

What's wrong with training managers? What's wrong is that you and other people who have the responsibility to deal with customers and suppliers day to day and, by phone, ear to ear are the ones who convey impressions to customers about the reliability, helpfulness, and quality of a company's services. Therefore, you should be trained, too.

To customers, you are the company.

To customers, you *are* the company. Performance of customer-contact professionals determines whether customers remain loyal. Your performance also determines how much customers buy and how often they buy it, when they *do* remain loyal.

Without training or education, a service professional may alienate one customer after another. They aren't likely to know what good service is! Most of them have never experienced good service in their lives. They have never *seen* good service. Some of them think that the consistently bad service they receive when *they* are customers is normal. They are wrong.

So, a logical question stands up and demands to be asked: How are rank-and-file employees supposed to learn how to provide good service? They can *educate themselves*. It is the best investment in success that any of them can make.

This is the rationale for the book you are holding in your hands. The book shows individual service professionals how to take the bull by the horns and reach for the stars. For over fifteen years I have been helping organizations provide the learning tools to improve the service skills of their entire work force.

Often front-line, they-do-the-work employees are not trained because the company expects them to quit soon. Executives reason that if they're trained, the money spent training them will have been wasted. So, they avoid wasting money by abstaining from training.

This thinking is an illustration of the classic self-fulfilling prophecy: A large part of the reason that turnover rate in service businesses is high — as high as 100 percent in retailing — is the fully-justified conclusion of front-line employees that their employers don't care about them, often because they don't train them. _This is the reason they quit._ They hadn't thought about quitting before.

Other executives who decide not to train service providers in customer service assume that everyone is born with the capacity if not the will to provide service. Therefore, managers reason, employees don't need to be *trained*, just put to work. They're wrong. Good service is not something that the average person learns by

Educate yourself. It is the best investment you can make in yourself.

The best service pros are simply outstanding employees.

participating in society, like they learn popular songs.

You won't find "Customer Service Techniques" listed in any course catalog for high schools, vocational schools, colleges, or universities that I know of. Yes, a few will offer it as part of their adult or continuing education, but not as part of their core curriculum. This is ridiculous since 90% of all the new jobs are in the service sector. Education has done a poor job of preparing people for the service jobs that exist.

I believe that service work is tied closely to just being a plain good employee. I believe that the best service pros are simply outstanding employees. Therefore, it makes sense to equip you, as a service provider, to build up your own job qualifications.

The *feelings* of customers need to be considered during every single contact with them. Even if we view our daily contacts with people on the job as routine and boring, we still need to consider their feelings. For them, contact with *us* may *not* be routine. Unfortunately, in our working lives we tend to think of the people we encounter as *strangers*. I suggest that you view on-the-job contacts as *opportunities* for developing friendships.

Many surveys prove that customers decide where to buy on the basis of their personal experiences buying. Sale prices, advertising, merchandising, location, products, and services attract customers only *once*. The *quality of personal relationships* is what brings them back. That's true of any contact with another person. We tend to avoid people with whom we have negative experiences.

Have you ever gone to a store with the intention of buying a specific item, then walked out of the store because you couldn't get anyone to wait on you? Have you ever avoided a restaurant because service was slow? Have you used an automatic teller machine to avoid impersonal, uncaring bank tellers? Have you tried to avoid an assignment at work because you didn't get along well with people assigned to help you?

In the end, price, taste, personal service, or importance of the project doesn't matter. *Feelings* matter. Read on for *more* ideas that will help you tune in, turn on,

View on-the-job contacts as opportunities for developing friendships.

If you are a pro in your work, a pro with a positive attitude and good work habits, prepare to make more money and be promoted faster.

and cash in for promotions, raises, and greater job satisfaction.

Quality service is an art and it must be *learned* in most new service sector jobs. That's true even of colleges and universities.

More than 600 colleges and universities use *Connections*, a customer service training tool that Service Quality Institute designed for Noel/Levitz Centers in Iowa City, Iowa that markets it. *Connections* is needed because many institutions of higher learning don't realize that students are *customers*, also.

This book presents methods for self-education in service and also for broad self-improvement in business and personal skills. Its objective is a promotion for you. Somebody's going to be promoted. It might as well be you.

Real pros get promoted before anyone else. If you are a pro in your work, a pro with a positive attitude and good work habits, prepare to make more money and be promoted faster.

Sharpen your skills and build up your motivation. Be ready when a promotion opportunity comes around — or be ready to apply for any better jobs that open up in your company. Whatever you do, don't wait for the organization to train or develop you.

Whatever you do, don't wait for the organization to train or develop you.

Section **I** *Self Improvement*

Self Development

You are a professional service provider. You are proud of your ability to deal smoothly with customers so they leave with smiles on their faces. But, sometimes you worry about getting ahead in this job. You sense that promotion depends to a large part on your job performance, your attitudes, and your job knowledge.

You feel that you do a good job and your boss tells you so. But, you have a feeling that you'd do better if you got some quality service training to improve your chances of "cashing in." Your company shows no signs of spending money to train you or any other service professional. Are

"The investment in learning on the job has contributed more to productivity increases over the past 40 years than technology, capital, and more than formal education."

Training magazine,
November, 1993

you going to sit in this job and spin your wheels until you go out and get another job that pays more?

Sometimes you get bored and down on yourself or the future seems bleak. You have trouble holding up your spirits. And then, one day, the flash bulb pops and you say aloud: "Well, if they aren't going to educate me, I'll *educate myself.*"

Successful people in any country in any age always have taken responsibility for themselves. They develop their qualifications and they reach for success. Today we call this behavior "pro-active."

A study conducted by the University of California revealed that the happiest and best-adjusted adults were those who took responsibility for themselves. Denis Waitley, in *Seeds of Greatness*, wrote: "Taking responsibility for your own...training is healthy and gratifying."

Start by making a strong commitment to yourself. Shake your fist above your head and shout out loud: "I'm going to *do it!*" If your determination is strong enough, you will *find* the time and money to do it.

Clarify your commitment by vowing to spend as much time and money developing your qualifications as you spend on your personal appearance. After a person graduates from school, typically no more than $1,000 is spent in a person's lifetime on personal and professional development such as adult education, seminars, tapes, and books. That's less than most people spend on personal appearance in one or two years. You also need to dress professionally. It impacts your self worth.

Each year set aside an amount of money that you can spare to train yourself. (This is your investment in *you*.) Then watch yourself recover training expenses in increased income. *This* is cashing in.

Look at it this way: If you really want to get promoted and make more money, you'll work at it. You'll welcome the *opportunity* to invest time and money on personal development. You'll stop off at the library after work one day a week. Tell the librarian what you want and you'll get all the help you need. Besides books and magazines you'll find video and audio tapes to check out and computers that simplify the process of requesting specific information from distant data bases.

The journey of a thousand miles starts with a single step.

Somebody is going to get promoted. It might as well be you.

Somebody is going to get promoted. It will be you if you clearly are the most knowledgeable, most skilled, and most determined person in your department.

Importance of Personal Development

Begin by deciding upon an objective or on several successive objectives such as the next several steps up in your job.

Most people seem to look at the positions in an organization as if they were organized in a pyramid shape. In the pyramid concept, many jobs and many promotions are available at the bottom, but there is little room at the top.

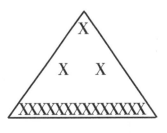

Cashing in involves aiming for the top.

I believe that the greatest opportunity exists *at the top*. That's because there's tremendous competition for the lower-level jobs. More people are competing for them. It will help if you will understand that your greatest opportunity is promotion to better jobs at higher levels. There's usually little opportunity competing for jobs that are merely *different*, near your same level. That's what everybody else does. *You* can be bold and self-confident and compete for the job *above* your level. That's where the greatest opportunity lays.

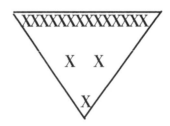

Cashing In involves aiming for the *top*. Fewer people are competing for the top positions. If you perceive that there is no opportunity in your organization for promotion beyond a certain point, then you are justified in establishing a specific position in another organization as one of your objectives.

Without objectives you are a locomotive without a track. You don't know where you're going. In this case reaching your objectives will be strictly accidental. However, if you think about your objective by visualizing, you set your sights and focus your mental camera. See it in your mind's eye in its colors, its feel, its fragrance, its sounds and its emotional resonance. Now you have direction. Now you have motivation. Now you have multiplied your chances for success in achieving your goal.

To activate yourself for pro-active pursuit of objectives, you must really *expect* to succeed. You must possess a powerful belief in yourself — a calm, clear, honest self-confidence. Close your eyes and actually *see* yourself a success.

You may be seated at a desk in your own office. You may be driving into a parking spot with your name on it. You may like the sound of people calling you "Mr." or "Ms." in a respectful tone.

Psychologist Maxwell Maltz wrote a very successful book on what he called "psycho-cybernetics." Dr. Maltz maintained that a strong emotional belief in yourself

Expect to succeed.

"As a man thinketh in his heart, so is he."

King Solomon

aligns your thoughts and efforts behind a drive to reach an objective. The message in his book is as valid today as when it was first written and is still referred to frequently by human development authorities. His book is a classic. Believing that it's so will make it so, Dr. Maltz taught.

Part of the success formula, then, is self confidence. Build your self confidence with "affirmations." An affirmation is the act of asserting (affirming) that a statement you make to yourself is true. It is a positive declaration that describes what you want to be, what you want to have, or how you want to live your life.

Repetition of such a positive thought over and over, day after day affects your subconscious mind. You begin to do things that promote those objectives that you have affirmed without even realizing what you're doing. You begin to live up to what you expect of yourself. Use this sample affirmation:

I am an intelligent, hard-working person and I'm positive that if I exert every ounce of effort at my command, I will:

Expecting success of yourself is far more constructive than continual fear produced by acute awareness of personal inadequacies, personal doubts, and fear of failure. Self-confidence is power. "The only thing we have to fear," said President Franklin Delano Roosevelt, "is fear itself."

Review the affirmations on the following pages and learn to use the positive affirmations, not the negative ones on the first page.

"The only thing we have to fear is fear itself."

President Franklin Delano Roosevelt

"It is never safe to look into the future with eyes of fear."

E.H. Harriman

NEGATIVE

- I hate myself.
- I wish I was dead.
- I'm going nowhere at work.
- It's just not my day.
- I just can't do this.
- Every time I try to talk to him (or her) we have an argument.
- I have a problem with my weight.
- I just know she (or he) won't like me.
- Why should I try? It probably won't work out anyway.
- I just can't seem to get caught up.
- I have the worst memory.
- I'm no good at...
- I never seem to get a break.
- Just this once won't hurt.
- I find something on sale and I can't help myself.
- I don't know what's wrong with me today.
- I've tried, but I just *can't*.

POSITIVE

- I like who I am.
- I'm glad to be alive.
- I'm making progress at work.
- Today is a GREAT day for me!
- I can handle this.
- Every time I talk to him (or her) we communicate even better.
- I am getting control of my weight.
- I just *know* she (or he) is going to like me.
- I am willing to try, there's a good chance it will work.
- I'm getting caught up on everything.
- I have an excellent memory.
- I'm good at...
- I'm fortunate that things go my way.
- Just this once I won't.
- Even if I find something on sale, I'm never tempted to spend what I shouldn't.
- I feel especially good about myself today.
- I'll keep trying and I'll GET IT YET!

Successful people see themselves from their high points in life.

You succeed or fail by the image you hold in your mind.

All of us would be better off if we learned a few simple "truths" about ourselves. These truths may sound strange, but they work! They can give you something extra to help you along the way.

Your truths could be worded something like this:

- I like who I am, and I'm glad to be me.

- I'm glad to be alive, and I've decided to be the best *me* that I can be.

- Today is a good day. Today is the day that I choose to be my best and to do my best. I'll have other good days, too, but today is special — and so am I!

- I've made the decision to win in my life. I'm in control, on top, in tune, in touch, and nothing can stand between me and the goals I've set for myself.

- I can do it. Just watch me and I'll prove it!

These are not the lofty words of a visionary. They are examples of simple, practical self-directions that can help you see yourself, and life around you, in a more effective way each day. It is very likely that these words, repeated often enough, indelibly etched in your mind, could have a powerful effect upon you.

Conscious thoughts and words are reflections of unconscious programs that create them. If your *conscious* self-directions are productive and healthy, and if they work for you, your *unconscious* self-directions also will be healthy and effective.

If your conscious self-directions are productive and healthy, and if they work for you, your unconscious self-directions also will be healthy and effective.

Self Concept

The greatest limitation you face is self imposed. You set your own ceilings.

If you think of yourself as a failure, you *will* fail no matter how hard you consciously try to succeed. You may accidentally outstrip your own self-image for a time, but you will quickly readjust.

If you cannot respect *yourself*, you cannot respect *others*, such as customers, nor can *others* respect *you*.

Isn't life just a series of choices? You can *choose* to be successful just as you can *choose* to fail by expecting failure. If you

The greatest limitation you face is self imposed.

set clear objectives, if your self confidence is a tower of power, and if in your own mind there is absolutely *no doubt* that you're going to succeed over time, then chances are *outstanding* that you will get where you are going.

A good feeling about yourself isn't something that happens just because you wish it would happen. You need to work at making it happen. The first step is to recognize that other people are not the ones who are primarily responsible when you do not feel good about yourself. You are responsible, all by yourself.

How often do you give yourself a pat on the back for a job well done? "Not often" is probably the right answer. Take a step back and *savor* your better moments. You need the solid emotional foundation that's established by self-praise to counter-balance the high winds of occasional failure or criticism.

Of course, others do have *some* influence upon the way we feel. Your good work is usually noticed, but it is not praised very often by co-workers or your boss. They figure that you are just doing what you're paid to do.

Self-praise is often difficult for us. It's difficult for many of us to say to ourselves: "You did a good job there, old boy." We're taught at an early age to be modest. We feel that praising oneself is conceited, and unnecessary. But, it is essential to success that you praise yourself *to* yourself. Doing so is one of the very effective means of maintaining your motivation. Your early influences toward modesty are misguiding you. You *need* "positive strokes" to equip yourself to repeatedly do your best work.

When the occasional compliment comes your way, accept it gracefully. If you act as if you didn't notice the compliment or if you dismiss it, you will appear to be a distrustful person. Or, you'll appear confused. Service professionals who love their jobs and who feel good about themselves will receive many positive comments from customers. You'd better be ready to receive these customer comments gracefully.

Studies show that we *feel* good about ourselves when we *look* good. When we're wearing nice clothes, have a nice hairstyle, are neatly groomed, or have lost weight, we feel good about ourselves.

You set your own ceilings.

If you don't control what you think about, somebody else will.

Other people, including customers, also take notice when we look good and are inclined to treat us in positive ways when we wear neat, clean clothing, our hair is well-groomed, our shoes are shined, and our fingernails are clean and clipped.

You can't count on receiving enough compliments from others to sustain your ego and to equip yourself, emotionally, to do good work. So, learn to compliment yourself. Complimenting yourself helps you deal with personal problems, too. And personal problems influence all parts of our lives, including our work lives. For instance, your ability to concentrate on your work will slip a bit when your spouse has just been laid off. You will be distracted by the realization that you don't have enough money to pay the rent tomorrow.

A self-compliment raises self-esteem and directly impacts performance. At the start of the day, say to yourself: "I feel good about myself," or "Today will be a great day!" Just worrying about problems doesn't solve them. Worry makes them worse. Most of what we worry about doesn't even come to pass.

Much of your success in dealing with customers and co-workers comes from success in dealing with yourself. The following quiz will help you identify what to compliment yourself on and what you need to improve on. In each category, circle the number for the statement that best describes your behavior or attitude. Make a rating for each item and total your ratings to review your evaluation.

One's attitude, not aptitude, is the chief determinant of success.

Quality Service Performance Standards

Instructions: In each category circle the number for the statement that best describes your behavior or attitude. Please make a selection for each item.

Attitude Toward Customers:
      1   Inconsiderate or indifferent
      2   Polite, but reserved
      3   Warm, friendly, and outgoing
Says "Thank You" and Smiles:
      1   Rarely
      2   Occasionally
      3   Always
Recognizes Customers:
      1   Doesn't remember customers
      2   Recognizes customers, but doesn't communicate
             those feelings to the customer
      3   Very good at recognizing customers with
             good facial expressions and verbal feedback
Uses Customers' Names:
      1   Doesn't know or call the customer by name
      2   Uses customers' names, but not often enough
      3   Remembers customers' names and
             pronounces their names correctly
Customer Oriented:
      1   Shy, uneasy with customers
      2   Helpful, but not completely comfortable
      3   Outgoing, helpful, and extremely comfortable

Customer Oriented Pressure Situations:

 1 Experiences frustration, usually makes
    no attempt at handling a situation

 2 Attempts to handle, then refers to a manager

 3 Attempts and usually succeeds in handling on own

Treats Customers as Being Real:

 1 Shows boredom and coldness

 2 Sometimes is tense, cold, and abrupt

 3 Always shows warmth and friendliness

Punctuality:

 1 Frequently late

 2 Usually on time

 3 Always prompt

Sickness/Lost Work Time: (per 30 day period)

 1 5 or more days gone

 2 2-4 days gone

 3 0-1 days gone

Reliability:

 1 Requires constant supervision

 2 Requires little supervision

 3 Requires no supervision

Attitude at Work to Supervisor and Co-workers:

 1 Resentful, aloof, or indifferent

 2 Helpful and cordial

 3 Motivated

Instructions:

 1 Can't follow instructions

 2 Does okay when instructions are repeated

 3 Follows instructions well

Work Habits:

 1 Poor work habits, does less than required

 2 Does only what is required

 3 Does more than required

Team Work:

    1   Does not contribute to team effort

    2   Has some ability, offers suggestions

    3   Talented and team motivated

Personal Appearance, Dress, and Uniform:

    1   Dress and personal appearance is not business acclimated

    2   Usually neat and tidy, needs to be more business acclimated

    3   Dresses appropriately and has good appearance

Personal Cleanliness and Hygiene:

    1   Poor, needs to improve

    2   Usually okay, needs to be more consistent

    3   Excellent habits

Initiative:

    1   Does only what is specifically outlined

    2   Requires supervisory guidance to be motivated

    3   Self-motivated, little or no supervision needed

Product or Job Skills Knowledge:

    1   Has limited knowledge, shows little interest

    2   Has some knowledge, interested in knowing more

    3   Knowledgeable

Listening Skills:

    1   Does not pay attention to customer needs

    2   Occasionally pays attention, needs improvement

    3   Asks good questions and pays attention to needs

Keeping Promises to Customers:

    1   Lacks follow-through on promises

    2   Usually remembers, needs improvement

    3   Good follow-through on promises

Positive Communication to Customers on a Daily Basis:

    1   Pays little attention, avoids compliments

    2   Gives compliments, needs to be more sincere

    3   Generous with genuine and sincere compliments

Positive Communication to Co-workers on a Daily Basis:
- 1 Pays little attention, avoids compliments
- 2 Gives compliments, needs to be more sincere
- 3 Generous with genuine and sincere compliments

Negative Communication to Customers:
- 1 Poor attitude, performance, and feedback
- 2 Normally good, needs to be more consistent
- 3 Rarely gives negative communication

Negative Communication to Co-workers:
- 1 Poor attitude, performance, and feedback
- 2 Normally good, needsto be more consistent
- 3 Rarely gives negative feedback

Ignores Customers/Absence of Quality Service Techniques:
- 1 Very poor, frequently ignores customers
- 2 Pays attention, but needs to use techniques daily
- 3 Pays attention, never ignores customers

Plastic Insincere Communication to Customers:
- 1 Communication is insincere and phony
- 2 Tries to be genuine, often perceived as plastic
- 3 Rarely plastic, very sincere and genuine

Handling Irate Customers by Using the Six Keys
to Cooling Down an Irate Customer:
- 1 Seldom, needs improvement
- 2 Usually, needs more practice
- 3 Very good, usually turns customers around

Ability to see Potential Problems and Stop Them
Before Customer Becomes Irate:
- 1 Ignores obvious problems
- 2 Uses the techniques, but not often enough
- 3 Uses the skills for defusing problems

Takes Responsibility for Legitimate Problems/Complaints:
    1   Defensive, tries to avoid blame
    2   Tries to use techniques, clumsy and inconsistent
    3   Effective at taking responsibility for legitimate complaints and turning the situation around

Accuracy of Performance:
    1   Very careless and sloppy performance
    2   Often inaccurate, occasionally makes mistakes
    3   Careful and consistently accurate

Quality of Work Performance:
    1   Poor and deficient quality of work
    2   Performs at average level of quality
    3   Places a high value on quality of work

Job Commitment:
    1   Shows lack of real job commitment
    2   Does an average job, but lacks commitment to superior job performance
    3   Dedicated commitment, does a thorough job

Doing More Than the Minimum for Others:
    1   Not helpful, tends to be rude and impatient
    2   Friendly, but needs to develop "put customers first" attitude
    3   Consistently gives more than the minimum to customers with pride and pleasure

Minimum Standards of Excellence with Customers and Co-workers:
    1   Inconsistent and unreliable at meeting personal standards of excellence
    2   Sets high standards, but is not consistent in meeting these standards with customers
    3   Sets high standards of excellence and has consistent habits of positive communication

Feels Good About Self:

1	Suspicious, distrustful, and unresponsive to receiving positive feedback
2	Likes self, but needs to feel more comfortable and receptive to receiving positive feedback
3	Likes self and is good at receiving and giving positive communication

Suggested Performance Evaluation

Rating	*Evaluation*	
1-51	Poor	Requires frequent close supervision and direction to achieve minimum job performance.
52-68	Marginal	Needs more customer service skill training.
69-81	Standard	Performs all aspects of the job and consistently meets customer service performance standards.
82-92	Excellent	Consistently exceeds requirements with superior quality and quantity. Starting to cash in. Should make more, get promoted and love job.
93-105	Superior	Demonstrates exceptional attitude, performance and ability. Obviously you love your job. Prime candidate for a promotion and ready to make more money.

4

How to be Successful

It's simple. Do your best and be honest with yourself. If you aren't doing your best, admit it so you can change your performance.

If you need a *reason* to do your best, money is a good one. You're likely to find yourself making more of it. Imagine the hike in income you'd see as a bell hop, wait person, cab driver or anyone else who received tips if you were always at your best. Just a smile and use of a customer's name might double your tips.

You could get *rich*! Just ask Jim Hernandez, the friendliest, most knowledgeable airport van driver in America, a genuine

*You could
get rich!*

customer service superstar. He pilots his van between New Orleans' Moisant International Airport and downtown hotels such as Hotel St. Marie. The book, *New Orleans, A Pictorial History*, lies on the hump in his van on every trip. He uses it to answer passengers' questions about the city when his memory bank is blank.

Another aspect of his helpfulness is the poll he takes of passengers to select the hotel they want to stop at first. As the van pulls away from the airport heading for the French Quarter and downtown hotels, Hernandez turns and says to his passengers over his shoulder: "Don't worry about paying. The ride is free, but you'll have to pay seven dollars to get your luggage back." Chuckle. Chuckle.

"Seat belts are available. I usually wear mine because I know how I drive." More chuckles.

He talks about entertainment events, telling people where they can find entertainment listings. And he never forgets to say, hoping that someone will hire him: "I'm a licensed tour guide. Inside me is a wealth of information dying to get out."

Additional benefits of superior personal performance are more friends and increased self confidence, the result of improved job performance and friendlier relations with customers.

Learning and practicing customer service — the job of every employee whether they deal face-to-face with customers or not — will improve your job performance *and* your personal relations outside of work. Many customer service practices are transferable to private life.

Learning and practicing customer service will improve your job performance and your personal realtions outside of work.

Here are other reasons to do your best on the job:

- To win a promotion

- To learn to love your job

- To learn a skill

- To gain experience that will look good on your resume

- To learn to deal with people

- To reach a goal

- To earn money

Do your best!

- To gain personal satisfaction

- To avoid boredom

- To lend variety to your life

Snap up every opportunity that comes along to make a contribution. Make suggestions for saving the company money, improving customer satisfaction, doing a job faster, and eliminating unnecessary work.

Attitude Determines Action

If you view a job as no more than a way to earn money so you can go out on Saturday night or buy nice clothes, you needn't simulate surprise when somebody else is promoted. Don't complain about unfair treatment.

Much disappointment on the job is a result of a poor attitude such as the expectation of fun and games instead of productive effort. People who are more interested in socializing than in high-quality job performance waste a lot of time trading stories and reporting what they did on their days off.

It's very difficult to win a promotion and make more money if you do not love your job.

Some people feel that doing a good job is not necessary: Showing up for work is all that's *necessary*. Also, too many people think that they don't need to love their jobs as long as the pay check is never late. Yet, they're interested in making more money. Here's a tip: It's very difficult to win a promotion and make more money if you do *not* love your job.

Customers don't *pay* for friendly service. They pay for merchandise or product "and that's all they're going to get. Good service is a bonus, and I don't feel like it today." Attitude determines action. If you tell your friends, "I hate my job," your work probably is low in quantity and quality. After a while you'll *really* hate your job.

It might make a big difference in your work life if you practice what has been called *self talk*. Just after your eye lids elevate in the morning, while you're still in bed, take a few seconds to think thoughts such as:

- "Today is going to be a great day! This might be the day that I get the big payoff for my hard work."

- "I feel smart and energetic today. I'm going to do some good work."

- "I enjoy finding new opportunities. Today I'm going to find another one."

- "I am a hard-driving person. Nothing can stop me unless I stop myself. I'll keep myself in motion today."

- "I look forward, never backward. Today I will be busy creating a bright and successful future. I know where I'm going. I'm well on my way."

Have you ever experienced this situation? You come to work all fired up. You start out energetic and enthusiastic, but soon everything starts going wrong because two people in your department called in sick.

Here's a case where self-talk works well. Tell yourself: "My responsibility is to do the best I can. That will be enough." Repeat the phrase now and then.

Visualization of top-notch personal performance receives a lot of attention in sports coverage. Sports psychologists instruct athletes in actually *seeing* them-

Nothing can stop you.

The way you see yourself often determines what you do.

selves performing in a superior way, in their minds' eyes.

When you distinctly *see* yourself doing fantastic work, then you *feel* that you are doing fantastic work. When you *feel* that way, you *perform* that way. The way we *see* ourselves often determines what we do. If you need proof, consider how well you work on a day after your boss has chewed you out compared with your performance the day after a raise. Different, right?

If your heart is set on a new car, mount a color picture of it on the wall in your work place. Glance at it occasionally. Sure as sunrises, you'll find a way to get that car sooner than you expected.

Psychologists explain the results of visualization by saying that our feelings determine our actions. Our actions determine whether we succeed or fail at any enterprise.

Before a performance, before a sales presentation, before a difficult confrontation, or before the daily challenge of meeting a goal, visualize that goal clearly, vividly, and relentlessly, over and over again.

Create an internal "comfort zone." Use visualization to become a customer service professional. Basically, visualize yourself doing and saying specific things associated with stellar customer service.

Of course, you must know what you need to do to practice outstanding service. If you work in a sales support department, visualize yourself processing orders faster, expediting delivery, and enhancing the *perceived* quality of your product with the high-quality service that you provide. Visualization can help you get a promotion or even get your own business!

Affirmation, on the other hand, is *self-talk*. Self-talk is consciously reprogramming your sub-conscious mind through the use of specifically-worded self-direction phrases. (You talk to yourself, don't you?) Psychologists say that people program themselves with sentences and phrases that they hear with their *mind's ear*. These statements create and reinforce conscious thoughts and words...and influence actions.

We live in a negative world. Television, radio, newspapers, and magazines feed us negative news. The people we work with

> *Self-talk is consciously reprogramming your sub-conscious mind through the use of specifically-worded self-direction phrases.*

Our actions determine whether we succeed or fail.

and associate with outside of work take their lead from the news angles used by the media. So, without constant self-talk, you will have trouble feeling good about the world and about your function in the world.

Our programming creates our *beliefs*. Our beliefs determine our *attitudes*. Our attitudes create our *feelings*. Our feelings determine our *actions*. The end result is that our actions determine whether we succeed or fail. *You* write this subconscious programming, thereby writing your life's script. If you write a script for a *successful* life, you'll be very likely to live a successful life.

You can go about your work talking yourself to success. (Don't move your lips unless you want a reputation for eccentricity.) You might even want to carry around index cards with sayings on them such as:

- "I am always enthusiastic."

- "I always smile and call people by their names."

- "I treat people the way I want to be treated." Or: "I treat people the way they want me to treat them."

- "I can answer any question about our product or service that a customer can throw at me."

- "I will go out of my way to make certain that a customer does not leave the premises angry at us."

Read the cards at least once a day. I started to use affirmations like this when I was 22 years old. They had a tremendous influence on my performance, income, and success. Some of my favorite affirmations are highlighted on the sides of the pages of this book.

Go out of the way to keep a customer.

Be Pro-Active

Decide that you're going to take steps to improve *your own* circumstances.

- Set standards and goals for yourself:

- Never compromise with honesty.

- Be orderly in person and in work.

- Listen twice as much as you speak.

- Help others succeed.

When I was 21 years old I began using goal-setting, affirmations, and visualizations that I learned from Success Motiva-

Look for ways to change.

tion Institute. I found that my success in life was directly proportionate to my application of the skills. Today the people who are able to convince themselves to change by learning new technology, new skills and procedures, and even new occupations and specialties will be the most successful in the fast-changing years ahead.

Look for ways to change. The key to the ability to change is a changeless sense of *who you are, what you are about*, and *what you value*. Here's where the mission statement comes in.

Some sample mission statement items are:

• Obtain the counsel of others.

• Develop one new competency or skill every year.

• Plan tomorrow's work today.

• Hustle while you wait. (Do something while you wait.)

• Keep a sense of humor and nurture it by using it every day.

- Don't fear mistakes. Fear only the absence of creative, constructive, and corrective responses to mistakes.

- Concentrate all abilities and efforts on the task at hand, not upon worrying about the *next* job or promotion.

- Be a self-starting individual who exercises initiative in accomplishing life's goals. Act on situations and opportunities, rather than waiting to be acted upon.

- Seize opportunities. Make them happen. Succeed. Enjoy success.

Seize opportunities.

Writing your *Personal Mission Statement* in terms of the important roles in your life gives you balance and harmony. It keeps each role clearly before you.

Review your roles often to make sure that you aren't totally absorbed by one role to the exclusion of others that are equally or even more important in your life.

After you identify various roles, then you can think about the long-term goals you want to accomplish in *each* role.

Self Image

If you don't *expect* much of yourself, you won't *deliver* much.

If you set goals that stretch your abilities, you'll deliver a lot because the challenge of higher achievement will motivate you. You'll be enthusiastic.

Nevertheless, don't go around setting goals that anyone would call unrealistic. A goal of election as United States Senator from your state won't accelerate your success. At least vow to become a senator in your state legislature first. The technique is to set reachable goals. Reaching them builds confidence that's helpful in achieving the next reachable goals.

Realize that you have a lot of untapped potential locked in you. Everyone does.

There is no doubt that when you set your goals high and fully expect that you've got what it takes to achieve them, it is amazing how much you can accomplish. It worked for me. I dreamed of becoming a millionaire by the time I turned 30 years old, and I did it. My father died when I was seven, and I grew up in a family with very little money. My mother always told me I could do better. She always made me feel good about myself. Fortunately, I believed her. I have always made goals and kept copies of them since I was 22 years old.

Set challenging (but not overwhelming) goals and devise a workable plan for reaching them. If you do, soon you will find that the success you *expect* is the success you *have*.

Realize that you have a lot of untapped potential locked in you. Everyone does. When you really believe that it's true, then your self-image will be strong and positive. You need that self-confidence to get a promotion or a raise — or both.

Be careful to avoid comparing yourself with other people. That's one of the principal reasons that many people's confidence takes to the ditch on the highway of life. Instead, compare what you *are* with what you have the *potential* to become.

I'll always remember the first time I listened to SMI's personal goal setting and leadership audio tapes. I stopped comparing myself to others and started to see myself as I could be. That advice motivated me to quit my first job after college and to go into business for myself.

I out produced my boss ten to one in sales. I asked for a forty percent raise but the organization procrastinated. I had been listening to the SMI audio tapes every day. They helped me see the potential I had within myself. I made the decision to quit one week after I received the raise, no matter how much it was. They gave me a twenty percent raise and I quit one week later to go into business for myself.

The first six months on my own I made $650, gross income before expenses. I didn't give up even though this was only a fraction of the money I was making previously. I taught *myself* how to sell, mastered the skills of goal setting, and

When you expect more of yourself, you accomplish more.

"No one can hurt you without your consent."

Eleanor Roosevelt, former First Lady

learned how to use affirmations and visualizations. I cashed in.

When you develop your untapped potential, and when you *expect* more of yourself, then you accomplish more...yourself.

It is our willing permission, our consent to what happens to us, that hurts us far more than what happens to us in the first place. Here are some important points about self confidence:

- Self confidence shows through and motivates confidence of customers in you.

- Personal self confidence is gained through practical know-how; know-how comes from knowledge and experience; and experience is gained by submitting yourself to obstacles and situations that others ordinarily shun. If you always avoid fearful situations, you miss the experiences from which you could best gain valuable know-how and, therefore, will fail to develop self confidence and positive expectancy.

- All of your feelings about yourself are based on the dictum: "Have a strong sense of self worth." Until you come to decide that you have intrinsic value as a human being, and that regardless of what others think or say, you're okay, you will never be able to reach your full *energy potential.* This is *the essence of a powerful life force* — a basic liking for yourself that enables you to make a contribution to the world, your society, and your family.

- Self confidence also comes from practical know-how; know-how comes from knowledge and experience; and experience necessarily involves confrontation and engagement. Self confidence helps us avoid the negativism that feeds upon itself, thereby decreasing confidence.

"They cannot take away our self respect if we do not give it to them."
Mahatma Gandhi, Hindu religious leader

 *Desire*

Did you ever want something so badly that you forgot to eat or drink while you attacked a goal. Sure you did. A burning desire transforms work into obsession.

Without strong *desire* you will not achieve *goals*, no matter how worthy they are or how workable your plan for achieving them. Desire comes from within. You can arouse it, stimulate it and control it.

You need a plan to reach a goal. Break down your goal into a series of steps that must be taken in order to achieve it. For each goal set a realistic deadline. Say to

Desire comes from within.

yourself: "I will *do* it." Then feel, see and hear yourself achieving the goal.

If you don't reach your goal, despite strong effort, just reevaluate yourself and the reality of your goal. Don't simply denounce yourself. Set a *new* goal. *Never* allow determination to reach your goals to be blocked by the resentful criticism of others. Rarely will others be cheering you on. That's why we have to master these skills of visualization, affirmation, and goals.

I have used the following MILLION DOLLAR PERSONAL SUCCESS PLAN by Paul Meyer, founder of SMI, for years. It works.

"The MILLION DOLLAR PERSONAL SUCCESS PLAN can be applied to every area of your life — spiritual, family, social, mental, physical, financial and career." — Paul J. Meyer

THE MILLION DOLLAR PERSONAL SUCCESS PLAN
by Paul J. Meyer, Founder, Leadership Management, Inc.®

I - Crystallize Your Thinking

Determine what specific goal you want to achieve. Then dedicate yourself to its attainment with unswerving singleness of purpose, the trenchant zeal of a crusader.

II - Develop a Plan for Achieving Your Goal, and a Deadline for Its Attainment

Plan your progress carefully; hour-by-hour, day-by-day, month-by-month. Organized activity and maintained enthusiasm are the well-springs of your power.

III - Develop a Sincere Desire for the Things You Want in Life

A burning desire is the greatest motivator of every human action. The desire for success implants "success consciousness" which, in turn, creates a vigorous and ever-increasing "habit of success."

IV - Develop Supreme Confidence in Yourself and Your Own Abilities

Enter every activity without giving mental recognition to the possibility of defeat. Concentrate on your strengths, instead of your weaknesses...on your powers, instead of your problems.

V - Develop a Dogged Determination to Follow Through on Your Plan, Regardless of Obstacles, Criticism or Circumstances or What Other People Say, Think or Do

Construct your Determination with Sustained Effort, Controlled Attention, and Concentrated Energy.
OPPORTUNITIES never come to those who wait...they are captured by those who dare to ATTACK.

9

How to be Your Own Teacher

You know what training and education you need to pave the road to success in *your* job. If you need help in identifying courses or sources of courses, see the Human Resources department, or talk to your boss.

The courses that you need might be taught at a vo-tech school, a junior college, or a college. (Inquire at the schools' scholarship offices about availability of scholarship assistance. Many scholarships are available if you are willing to take time to find them.) Perhaps your company even rebates all or part of the tuition cost.

If you won't take a chance on yourself, you haven't got a chance.

Some correspondence courses are also available through the mail. Ask the Human Resources department, or ask a librarian for a directory of correspondence schools.

If you can round up fifteen or more employees in your company to take a customer service training course, contact Service Quality Institute. SQI offers courses customized to many different business categories that are designed for groups. SQI has distributors, consultants, and licensees throughout the world who can be of help.

Self-improvement audio tapes can be played in your car on your trips between home and work, repeatedly. You can even listen to them on the bus or subway through head phones! Listen to the same tapes five or six times to reinforce their messages.

To obtain personal development, leadership, affirmation, and visualization learning programs, contact Success Motivation Institute in Waco, Texas at 817-776-1230 and ask for a local distributor in your area.

Above all, commit yourself to reading magazines and books. If you want to read faster, call your local School District office or the United Fund and ask where you can go to enroll in a reading program. Or, obtain the speed reading program offered by Dennis Paulson of Power Reading in Canada.

If you *can* read and you don't read, re-member this: The person who doesn't read is no better off than the person who can't read. If you have a home computer, it will present you with all the reading you can handle. The electronic data base ser-vices that you can hook up to your com-puter via your phone line contain current information on *your* field.

The leading computer on-line services are: Prodigy, CompuServe, GEnie, America On-Line, Delphi, and Applelink. Look them up in the phone book if you wish to subscribe.

Read trade magazines that you see at work and note addresses of organizations that offer information that expands upon the content of articles. Among articles in the trade magazines, you'll see advertis-ing for audio or video training tapes,

Commit yourself to reading.

Avoid model-ing yourself after people who are less successful than you.

books, or training courses and seminars that will help you succeed.

In the unlikely case that no one in your company subscribes to any of these magazines, suggest to your boss or to the Human Resources department that the company subscribe to them.

Finally, remember this: Associating with people you respect who are more success-ful than you will help you stay on the course toward success. There's no value to you in settling for being a big fish in a small pool. Share someone else's vision. This could be the person in the company that most people consider to be the best at customer service. Avoid modeling yourself after people who are less success-ful than you. They are likely to put you down, considering you to be self-impor-tant or arrogant.

10

The Win-Win Paradigm

Cooperation in the workplace is as important to you as *competition in the marketplace* if you want to become known as a person who gets things done.

The win-win philosophy of personal relationships at work is an alternative to win-lose: I win. You lose.

Win-lose is "my way, not your way" and "my way or no way." *Win-win* is a better way — a higher way. Both parties win!

Win-win maximizes cooperation. You feel good and the other person feels good. It's possible to work together, cooperatively, to the benefit of both of you.

A service professional always lets the customer win.

In a win-lose situation, the win usually is a short-term win and the loser carries around battle scars and a desire to win next time. A service professional always lets the customer win. Remember your goal is to keep the customer, not to prove who is right or wrong. That's your win.

When two determined, stubborn, ego-invested win-lose people interact, the result is *lose-lose*. Both become vindictive and want to *get back* or *get even*. In the long run, if both parties don't win *something*, both parties lose. You win more of what you want by going for what you *both* want. Don't let your ego get the best of you. A pro makes the customer and fellow employee feel good.

Win-win is a frame of mind and a state of being that seeks mutual benefit as a result of all human interaction. Win-win means that agreements or solutions are mutually beneficial, mutually satisfying. With a win-win solution, all parties feel good about a decision and are committed to the action plan.

In a win-win world, life is *cooperative*, not competitive. You should be aware that personal character (your character and the character of people that you deal with on the job) is the foundation of win-win.

Three character traits are essential in win-win — integrity, maturity, and abundance mentality. You know what integrity and maturity are.

Abundance mentality needs explanation. It is the state of mind that assumes that there is plenty out there for everybody. Just because you win doesn't mean that someone else loses. It is perfectly possible to arrange things so that everybody wins. Bickering and win-at-all-costs behavior is not necessary. It's also undesirable because it is usually counter-productive. That is, you do *not* get a raise and you do *not* receive a promotion.

An important part of the win-win mentality is accepting responsibility. Admit mistakes and you will mark yourself as an uncommon person, indeed. (You don't often hear someone say: "That was my fault. I was wrong.")

If you make a mistake at work or if you are mean and vindictive toward a co-worker, accept responsibility for your error. Don't blame it on someone or some-

Admit mistakes and you will mark yourself as an uncommon person.

In the customer's eyes, you represent the entire organization.

thing else such as staying up too late. Instead, say this: "I'm wrong. I made a mistake. It was my fault." Obviously this is the skill of a service professional. This technique also works great at home with your family.

In 25 years of sales, management, and consulting I can count on the fingers of one hand the number of times I've heard a person say "I made a mistake. It's my fault." It's *magic*. It really works with customers! Be careful, though. This may cause a few customers to have heart attacks out of shock. Usually they are so overwhelmed that you would say this, you take the wind out of their sail. As a result they almost always accept your apology.

When you directly accept responsibility for a wrong perceived by a customer or fellow employee, you put yourself in a strong leadership position. Remember the customer is not blaming you personally. In the customer's eyes, you represent the entire organization. You just bore customers when you put responsibility onto a computer, another department or a supplier.

After you accept responsibility, do everything in your power to correct the wrong. Learn to *think* win-win. In every interaction with anyone else on the job, consciously look for a way that *both* you and the other person can win.

It is also important that you establish a win-win relationship with your supervisor, if you want a raise or promotion, or if you prefer to like your work. If you try hard to get along and your boss still treats you like an idiot who can't be trusted without close supervision, it may be time to look for another job. Don't quit your present job before you have another one, though, or before you have done everything you can think of to succeed in your present job.

Don't overlook the possibility of transfer to another position in the same company — or even to a new position. High performance will stand out...and be rewarded. In some instances, service professionals can create new positions for themselves or win promotion to positions in other departments.

Simply giving yourself enough time on a job to master it, thereby putting yourself

Learn to think win-win.

*High perform-
ance will
stand
out...and be
rewarded.*

in position to be promoted, will lead to success. I review many job applications from people who go through two to four jobs a year. They are never hired.

11

Pursue Self Improvement Aggressively

Begin by making a resolution: "I will enthusiastically accept all the training that's available from my employer." In some companies earnest employees on the move will get very well educated that way. In other companies the result of *making* such a resolution would be exactly the same as *not making* the resolution, because there is no training available.

In this case, you'll need to train yourself. In 1969, when I was 21 years old, I paid $500 of my own money for *The Dynamics of Personal Leadership*, the personal development program developed by Paul Meyer of Success Motivation Institute. It

*Being
unsuccessful
is a waste
of time.*

improved my self concept, helped me set my goals, and created an intense desire to succeed.

Make suggestions. Some companies pay a bonus for suggestions that save or make money. If you want to generate ideas, maintain an active mind by exercising it. Identify your interests, and then read about them, do them, and watch videos in which others are doing them. If your mind is alert and searching, you will do high-quality work and it will boost your chances for a higher pay rate and promotion.

The community college near you probably sends you a schedule of hundreds of evening classes. Pick a self-improvement class that's job related and spend one night a week on personal development. Junior colleges, colleges, and universities in your area also offer night classes. Call the continuing education department or extension division of the local college or university and ask them what courses are available in your field.

If you try, you might find that you really could afford at least one self-improvement class. These expenses are tax de-

uctable if spent to improve your position or get a new job. Some companies will even pay for classes! More than 90 percent of employees eligible for company tuition-support plans do *not* use them. Those are all employees that you can leap-frog on the way to a promotion if you just spend a fraction of your time on education and self-improvement.

Some companies will even pay for classes!

If you're willing to work at it, you can find many opportunities for self-improvement. I have listened to audio tapes and read an average of one self-improvement book per month since I was 21 years old. I've accumulated quite a library in a quarter century. The safest investment you or I can ever make is in ourselves, developing our minds. This is how we cash in. I now read over 24 self improvement books a year. Two or three good ideas make it worthwhile. In every book, I highlight the key ideas, grade the book, and put in the date I completed it.

Home study courses are also still available. Many of them combine video or audio instruction (and now CD-ROM and interactive computer discs) with printed workbooks and manuals. Courses are keyed to the interests of the television

The safest investment you can ever make is in yourself.

and high-tech communication generation. You probably already own a VCR, so just pop in one of these self improvement videos and get educated instead of bored by staring at commercial television.

One of the secret weapons for individuals who take personal responsibility for developing their success is the Instructional Systems Association (ISA). Its 130 members offer instruction in far more than 130 subject areas. They represent the top training companies in the United States. Contact ISA and tell them your objectives. They'll direct you to a member who has a system or program that will meet your needs. You can reach ISA at P.O. Box 1196, Sunset Beach, CA, 90742. Phone: 714-846-6012. Fax: 714-846-3987.

Certainly, the training costs something; but, you can be sure that the cost is much less than formal college or vocational school education. The instruction is also much more practical and more directly applicable to the everyday world of work.

The National Speakers Association (NSA) has some 6,000 members, many of whom produce audio and video cassettes —

some of them on topics that can help *you* cash in. If you have heard or have been referred to a speaker such as that, call NSA and obtain the speaker's address and phone number. The NSA can be reached at 1500 S. Priest Dr., Tempe, AZ, 85281. Phone: 602-968-2552. Fax: 602-968-0911.

And then there's just plain reading. Many people don't do it anymore; so here is another fruitful source of education waiting to be plucked off the tree of life...by *you*. The National Council of Teachers of English has found that although most Americans can read, the majority of them don't read books. Furthermore, the average American reads only one magazine regularly. According to the American Newspaper Publishers Association, most American families don't subscribe to daily newspapers, either.

Begin with a book-a-month objective. Then try to read one self-improvement book every two weeks. The least expensive route to self improvement is reading books and listening to self-help audio tapes. You can obtain many of these at your local library. If you can't find what you want there, buy them at a book store

The least expensive route to self improvement is reading.

If you have the passion, you will read broadly.

or send for them through the mail. Zig Ziegler, America's most successful and popular motivational speaker, spends three hours a day reading.

People *can* be motivated. They *can* be eager to succeed. And they *can* be consumed by a passion for success. If you have the *passion*, you will read broadly and expose yourself to the most respected thinkers in your field, whether your field is antiques, virtual reality, fast food, or medical appliances.

12

How to Get Noticed

What *is* customer service?

There is a service element in any activity pursued by any employee because, ultimately, all activity impacts the real or perceived quality of the product that the customer buys. Service is selling, warehousing, delivery, inventory, order selection, adjustments, correspondence, billing, credit, finance, accounting, advertising and public relations, data processing, and new product development.

For *you*, customer service is whatever the customers that you deal with think that it is. The "customers," for those of you who don't deal directly with customers may be

In the service culture, everyone has a customer.

members of the staff who deal directly with customers. Your role is to equip *them* to provide good service. In the service culture, everyone has a customer.

Service, more than almost anything else, is a good attitude. Why is attitude important? Because if you happen to think that you aren't anyone's servant and, therefore, you aren't going to serve, then you are likely to make some customers mad. That's not good for your future in a service economy.

Another attitude that can harm your chances for success results in *assuming* the intention or capability of a customer. You assume that a customer you see wandering down the aisle isn't going to buy anything because they can't buy or won't buy. You assume that the customer is too young to be a customer, too poor, probably not the decision maker in the customer group in which she or he is moving.

What's wrong with this attitude? It's often wrong. Ever hear of the woman dressed like a bag lady who was so insulted by the neglect of a service worker that she bought the company? (So what's the first thing she did after she became the new owner?)

Service is a skill. Some even call it a talent. Service is professionalism. It's an art. Look upon service as merchandise that you *deliver* to customers, if that helps you vault the *service-is-demeaning* hurdle.

Others are hung up on the thought that people who buy from them should get the merchandise, or they should get the service. Information, assistance, friendliness...those are *extras*, not really earned by customers. Fortunately, this has become a discredited concept. Today's customer service professionals honor the concept of service expressed in: thoughtfulness, courtesy, integrity, reliability, helpfulness, efficiency, availability, friendliness, knowledge, and professionalism.

The most important ingredient of professional service delivery probably is treating customers as *special*,thereby developing friendly relationships with them. When you treat people as special, they usually treat you the same way. You like that. Life moves more smoothly. You have fewer problems on the job. Your personal life

Service is a skill.

It is far easier to create a positive impression than it is to erase a negative one.

improves. You can make this happen by positive communications, such as: praise for a good job, a friendly smile, and many "thank you" replies.

Anyone who consistently receives positive feedback feels good about the person giving the feedback. They also feel good about themselves. When you receive *negative* communication, you react in the opposite way — with resentment.

Think about your experiences as a customer. Have you ever been ignored when you tried to get help in a bank? A drug store? A supermarket? How did you feel as you stood there feeling invisible? How did you feel when you called that business and sighed and doodled while listening to several successive transfers until you were transferred to the last resort...who was on vacation?

It is far easier, we know, to create a positive impression than it is to erase a negative one. That is, customers must experience a lot of excellent service before they forget one insult. By consistently providing quality service we create positive relationships. This not only helps us and the people we deal with, but it helps the entire organization.

So, you see, you have an important job. It's important because quality customer service often turns failure into success for many companies in the service society.

The following is a sample plan for service success.

Quality service often turns failure into success.

PERSONAL SUCCESS PLAN FOR EXCELLENCE IN CUSTOMER SERVICE

by John Tschohl, President, SERVICE QUALITY INSTITUTE

I. Feel Good About Yourself

When you know that you are doing your best for customers and work associates you will feel good.

II. Practice Habits of Courtesy

Forgetting to be courteous signals indifference and arrogance. The more courtesy you give, the more courtesy you receive.

III. Apply Positive Spoken Communication

Positive communication conveys the gift of good feelings. Your words are evidence of your thoughtfulness.

IV. Perform for Customers

Customers have a right to expect good service. Their money buys that right.

V. Listen Carefully

Concentrate on each customer. Tune in to their needs and attitudes. Anticipate. Read between the lines. Ask questions to show that you care.

VI. Learn and Grow in Your Job

Every day you have a choice: Grow or decline. If you choose to grow in your work, learn about your customers, learn about your products and services, learn about your company, and learn to do your job even better. The result will be a warm feeling of self fulfillment. (That, too, is *cashing in*.)

Section **II** *Service Improvement*

A Rockefeller Foundation study discovered that an astonishing 68 percent of all customers stopped buying from companies because of the indifferent way they were treated. Marketing Sciences conducted a survey and found that people want to be treated as individuals. They want to be noticed and appreciated.

Here's a tip for any person intent upon getting ahead in a service society.: Treat people as potential *friends*, not as demanding *customers*. Customer service is largely a matter of good relationships with customers. Customers are people. When you treat customers the way you treat your personal friends, you'll be good

As far as customers are concerned, you are the company.

at customer service. Better yet is the *Platinum Rule*: "I treat people the way they want me to treat them."

Employees who deal with customers need people skills ---- the interpersonal knowhow to handle a universe of customer attitudes and diverse situations, and to uncover and address needs. Employees must leave customers with the feeling they are in good hands.

Establish trust between you and your customers by greeting them and responding to their needs. Customers want to feel that they can depend on you. If you can do this, then you have a great future in today's service society. Expect job offers from other service organizations if you maintain your employability, become a superior customer service professional, and do not become a job hopper.

Remember: As far as customers are concerned, *you* are the company. You are probably their only human contact at the company on a particular day. Engage customers in conversation and listen for needs that may not be obvious. Ask questions to determine whether the customer needs more information about your product or service or whether they are concerned about delivery.

Each customer you deal with has different service needs. Whatever their needs, they expect to deal with individuals who have positive attitudes and who treat them with courtesy and respect.

Respond to customer needs by offering effective solutions. By knowing your job, you can either help customers yourself or you can refer them to a team member who can help them. That means that you must be familiar with services available. Perceiving their needs signals to customers that you want them to enjoy their experiences with you and encourages them to return.

Perceiving their needs signals to customers that you want them to enjoy their experiences with you and encourages them to return.

13

Self Image

People react quickly to the image that you project. If you greet people by name, compliment them, or thank them for their purchases, you will get a positive reaction. Names are magic. Get a customers name from a check or credit card. Or, introduce yourself by name, a move that often prompts customers to volunteer their names.

I am amazed at the few people who practice this brand of personal service. If you do, you will be as conspicuous as a coyote running down Main Street — to customers *and* to your boss.

Names are magic.

You must, however, always be sincere. If you are just faking sincerity, customers will know it. They have an insincerity detector that's effective at thirty feet. Sometimes we make comments like this without thinking, and out of repetition, they come off very plastic and insincere.

When a customer that you know comes in, greet the person by name. Smile. Maintain eye contact. Again, this is cashing in. Master these skills and you will love your job, make more money, and get a promotion.

During the next week keep track of the number of times that customer service people whom *you* buy from greet you by name, smile, and look at you directly. I predict that no more than five percent of them will perform in this manner.

Calling customers by name is an important part of building positive relationships. Doing so shows respect and suggests recognition, openness, and friendliness. Once you have a customer's name, don't forget it. If necessary, write it down in a record that you keep just for this purpose. Consult your record as long as you can't remember the name.

If your contact with people is over the phone, jot down the caller's name as soon as it is mentioned. Then work it into the conversation whenever doing so seems natural. Don't worry about using the name too often. Most people never tire of hearing their name spoken. Here are a few possible greetings that you can use when you approach customers in person or on the phone.

Using names shows respect and suggests recognition, openness, and friendliness.

"Hello!"

"Good Morning!"

"Thanks for calling!"

"How may I help you?"

"Are you enjoying the beautiful weather?"

"Is there something in particular you are looking for?"

"That is certainly a pretty color, Mrs. Morton."

Initiate conversation. Find out how the day is going for the customer. Comment on their workload, their fine appearance — anything that conveys the accurate

If the customer doesn't win, neither you nor the company wins.

impression that you are friendly, considerate, and interested in them. After you've done this for a while you'll find that it's easier and easier to do because people respond positively to you, and that's a benefit for you.

As a service provider you should be dedicated to win-win situations, described earlier. It's not only you and the company that should win. The *customer* should win at the same time! If the customer doesn't win, neither *you* nor the *company* wins. Most companies set up fail-safe relationships with customers and there is *no way* that the company can lose.

Your customers may have different personalities, come from different parts of town, or belong to different socio-economic groups. Regardless of their backgrounds, they want to be treated fairly and equally.

Your hard work at developing relationships with customers has a high payoff potential. You develop an *emotional bank account* that helps you get ahead. You earn the *deposits* into this emotional bank account with continuous superior performance, courtesy, kindness, honesty, and commitments that you keep.

You can build up a useful reserve of good will and trust in your emotional bank account and, if necessary, you can call upon that trust to compensate for mistakes. If you practice bad habits of discourtesy, disrespect, interrupting, overreacting, ignoring, or threatening, eventually you will receive an overdraft notice.

Then you'll be in trouble. If you are not customer-centered, you will feel as if you are walking on mine fields, careful of everything you say and do, measuring every word.

Your hard work at developing relationships has a high payoff-potential.

14

*Being A
Good Listener*

Service Quality Institute (SQI) emphasizes *active listening*. Employees are taught to clear their minds of thoughts and listen *actively* to every customer. They learn to ask open-ended questions to facilitate an indepth analysis of the customer's needs and desires. SQI is an international service consulting and training organization that produces the *Feelings* quality service training program for employees and a variety of training programs on quality service for executives, managers, and employees.

Among other steps in active listening is paraphrasing what the customer says.

The deepest need in every human being is the desire to be appreciated.

"You say that the shipment scheduled to arrive on Friday hasn't arrived yet?"

"It's the blue with the countersunk rivets that you want, then?"

"Size 11D, you say? Give me just a minute and I'll find it."

Ask questions to obtain missing information.

Once you have obtained information about the needs of your customers, show that you understand by restating what you've heard. Repeat the information and ask if the statements are correct. This avoids misunderstandings and leads to exceptional service.

When you listen, really listen, to a customer, you raise the customer's self-esteem by demonstrating interest in what he or she is saying. When you listen you say: "You are important to me. I appreciate you." That makes a customer feel good and puts him or her into a buying frame of mind. Famed psychologist William James said that the *deepest need* in every human being, including service providers, is the desire to be appreciated.

The idea behind listening, in customer service, is to actually hear what customers say. *Appearing* to hear is not good enough. I am amazed at how many service employees ask a question and have no intention of listening to the answer. You know because they ask the same question again and again.

To be a good listener, concentrate on the customer. Tell your mind: "Stay focused. Don't wander away." Maintain a positive attitude. You really *want* to hear what the customer is saying so that you can react and generate a satisfied customer.

The world would be a better place if customers would return the favor and do for service providers what they expect service providers to do for them. One waitress represented the views of millions when she said: "I can tell countless stories about customers not listening to me, even when I ask a question!"

If you haven't found out by now you'll find out soon that few customers compliment you, even if you deserve a compliment. That's why you should learn to compliment yourself with affirmation and self talk.

Appearing to hear is not good enough.

Be willing to let customers talk.

Here is a listening technique that's valuable for customer service employees. "The Golden Pause" was originated by Lyman K. Steil, PhD, "The Ambassador of Listening" and a former University of Minnesota professor.

Dr. Steil advocates this: When a customer has finished a statement, pause for three to four seconds. This gives you, the employee, time to absorb what was said and to think of a good response. Dr. Steil guarantees dramatic improvement in the quality of the listening process when this device is used. The human mind accomplishes a great deal in those three to four seconds.

Besides these specific tactics, certain attitudes and behaviors are useful in improving listening in the employee/customer situation.

- Be courteous to the customer instead of aggressively trying to dominate the customer in conversation. Avoid "the terrible compulsion" (Steil) to demonstrate how well you speak.

- Be willing to let customers talk.

- Put energy into your listening. Look like an active listener, not like a person who's been awakened three hours before the alarm clock rings.

- Find something to be interested in, whenever a customer speaks.

- Respond in some way. Nod your head. Say "Uh-huh." Convey to the customers that you are interested in what they are saying and even enjoying it.

Dr. Steil and colleagues, Larry Barker and Kittie Watson, suggest specific techniques for listening in their book, *Effective Listening: Key To Your Success* (McGraw-Hill, 1983).

A good listener, of course, is well-equipped to develop essential good relationships with customers. To be successful in meeting the needs of others you must first understand them. That's where listening comes in. Be aware that understanding people does not come naturally. However, it is an ability possessed by every successful customer service professional.

Put energy into your listening.

Listen with the intent to understand.

People are born wanting to be understood. They must work at putting customers first — work at really wanting to understand *their* needs and wants. It is not very common for people to listen with the intent to *understand*. They listen with the intent to *reply*. They're either speaking or preparing to speak. They're filtering everything through their own needs, reading their autobiographies into other people's lives.

- "Oh, I know exactly how you feel!"

- "I went through the very same thing. Let me tell you about my experience."

They project their own home movies onto other people's behavior. They prescribe their own glasses for everyone with whom they interact. If they have a problem with someone — a son, a daughter, a spouse, an employee — the reason for the problem, they think, is that the person "just doesn't understand."

Next to physical survival, the greatest need of a human being, including service providers, is psychological survival to be understood, to be affirmed, to be validated, to be appreciated. This was a tenet of John Dewey, a twentieth century United States educator and philosopher. He believed in learning by experience and motivation by a sense of human need. This is a reality that, once realized and put into action, can make your fortune.

Unfortunately, many people working in the service field view customers as unwelcome interruptions in an otherwise pleasant day. They should treat customers as friends instead of as antagonists and annoyances. Treat them as if they sign their paycheck, if that makes it easier for them to be courteous.

When you listen to a customer with empathy, you are, believe it or not, making a contribution to that person's psychological survival in life. Once you've done that, you've earned a smile (even if you can't see it). A browser becomes a customer...or a better customer...or a more loyal customer.

For you, the payoff is a raise or a promotion...or job satisfaction, that is nothing to sneeze at, either.

Treat customers as friends instead of annoyances.

15

Handling Complaints

Relationship building is one thing. Relationship salvage is another thing — a more difficult challenge.

An angry customer is *not* necessarily destined to become a former customer. If you *quickly* solve a problem that's ruining a customer's day, the customer will return 95 percent of the time. A study for the U.S. Office of Consumer Affairs that uncovered this statistic also determined that if a complaint is resolved, but not necessarily *quickly*, between 54 and 70 percent of customers who register complaints will still do business with an organization.

If you quickly solve problems that ruin customers' days, they will return 95% of the time.

Don't just react to anger with anger. You have the *freedom* to choose how you will act and react. When a customer screams at you, it is not written anywhere that you *must* scream back. Nor is it written that service providers *must* forever smile and say "Yes, Ma'am" or "Yes, Sir" forever without any recourse to pride or self respect. Restrain yourself; then set out to change an angry face to a happy face by practicing these techniques:

Acknowledge a mistake immediately, correct it, and learn from it. Or, take responsibility for the problem even if it's not your fault by apologizing for anyone's error or oversight.

Make it obvious to the customer that helping in this difficult situation is your most important priority.

Listen carefully. *Look* like you're listening. Practice in front of the mirror, if you want to be a real professional.

Ask questions to clarify details. Show your concern. Try to understand the problem. Identify the exact nature of the problem, restating what you're told. This behavior is easier when you realize that a complaint is a request for help, not a reflection on you, personally.

Focus a courteous and helpful attitude on the customer. By *acting* on a problem you remain in control of the situation, thereby usually turning an initial failure into an ultimate success.

When you discover the cause, explain it to the customer in calm, factual terms.

Ask the customer what he or she feels should be done to correct the problem. Offer solutions that meet the needs of the customer or find someone who can.

If the best solution lies outside the limits of your abilities to correct the problem, immediately contact your supervisor for help.

When possible and necessary, follow up with a phone call or hand written note.

When dealing with angry customers, keep these "don'ts" in mind:

Don't challenge the customer's honesty.

A complaint is a request for help, not a reflection on you, personally.

The customer is always right.

Don't wander away from the specific problem.

Don't find fault. "The customer is always right" is a fine motto, even if the customer is wrong.

Don't let your emotions prevent you from doing what you know must be done.

Whatever you do, do *not* tell a customer that he or she is "wrong." A new car dealer's customer service representative said that to me once. As a result, the dealer lost about $56,000 in business.

Here's how we got to the point where the customer service rep stuck his foot in his mouth.

I once owned a Buick Riviera. The battery was constantly running down and had to be recharged three to five times every week. I took it in to my Buick dealership where they said they had fixed the problem. They gave me a bill for $195 to prove it.

A month later I was forced to face the fact that I'd wasted $195. The problem had not changed. So, *again* I took the car in to the dealership. This time I said: "Why don't you check out the battery." Surprisingly, they listened to me. A couple hours later they called and said: "You were right. The problem *was* the battery. You need a new one."

The trouble is that they wanted to charge me $25 for touching a tester to the battery to determine that it wouldn't accept a charge from the alternator. I refused to pay. They said if I wanted my car I had to pay the $25. The customer service manager said: "We want to keep you as a customer, so we'll give you credit for $25 for future work...even though you are wrong."

The affect on my body temperature was the same as the affect of a can of gas thrown on a fire. As I hung up the phone I was vowing to *never* return to the dealership.

It happened that during the next twelve months I had three auto accidents. (I probably had a case of long-term distraction caused by the dealer's behavior.) The average cost of repairs was $4,500 — a total of about $13,500. That was business that the Buick dealership did not receive.

Whatever you do, do not tell a customer that he or she is "wrong."

*What you do
for others
lives forever.*

Two years later, my wife had her heart set on an Isuzu automobile. It happened that this Buick dealership also sold Isuzus, but we drove eight miles beyond the offensive dealer to buy the car from a different dealership.

This last year, we wanted a Mazda. The same management firm also owned a Mazda car dealership. Instead of returning to this dealer, we bought a car from a dealership seven miles away.

16

It's Not What You Say But How You Say It

That's not *entirely* true, but it's almost true. Researchers estimate that about 90 percent of the content of a communication consists of cues *other than words*. Body language, vocal and other cues send an estimated 4,000 intelligible messages during a typical day. Perhaps this is why the hearing impaired often are exceptional at sensing speech, even if they can't read lips.

When you stand there speaking with a customer, you are *speaking* mostly without words — non-verbally. That's why people who despise customers and hate being of service to *anyone* can have such a devastating impact upon a company's

Body language, vocal and other cues send an estimated 4,000 intelligible messages during a typical day.

business. (They shouldn't be hired in the first place.)

Their disdain for customers shows as clearly as a spaghetti stain on a white blouse. They often wear an expression that comedian George Carlin called DIL-LIGAD: "Do I look like I give a damn?" (The answer is "No.") Even if you aren't aware of it, you *speak* to customers with your:

- Posture: Slouching or crossing your arms across your chest conveys boredom or anger.

- Facial expressions: A smile lets customers know you are happy to see them.

- Gestures: Expansive gestures show interest.

- Tone of voice: Volume, pitch, pace of speaking, and vocal inflections all influence the words you are saying.

- Eye contact: Eye contact usually means increased comfort and trust.

- Mannerisms: Tapping your fingers indicates impatience or resentment.

As Sigmund Freud said: "He that has eyes to see and ears to hear may convince himself that no mortal may keep a secret. If his lips are silent, he chatters with his fingertips; betrayal oozes out of him at every pore."

If you look neat and clean, customers judge your appearance as a sign of concern and responsibility. A good posture, smile, eye contact, and attentiveness are all positive examples of body language that build confidence between you and your customer.

Some taxi drivers can profit by learning this lesson. Many wear shirts too small for their portly frames so the shirts bulge open between buttons. Stubble on their chins; long, tangled hair; body odor; and dirty fingernails conspire to give riders the feeling that they're passengers in the only taxi serving the Black Hole of Calcutta.

These cabbies would be more successful clean-shaven, with neatly-trimmed hair, sharp creases in their shirts and pants, and a shower just before their shift begins. They must also wear a smile to complement their professional appearance.

Good posture, a smile, eye contact, and attentiveness are all positive examples of body language that build confidence between you and your customer.

Consider Yourself Empowered

At Nordstrom's department stores employees are given carte blanche to fulfill the one overriding rule on the sales floor: The customer *must* leave satisfied.

When Edwin Hoffman was chairman and chief executive of Woodward & Lothrop, a wellknown Washington, DC department store, he was shopping at Nordstrom's Westside Pavilion store in Los Angeles. A problem arose, and the saleswoman offered to place a longdistance call for him on Nordstrom's tab. "A tear came to my eye," said Hoffman.

Rule No. 1:
The customer
is always
right.

Consider how much Federal Express has benefited from word-of-mouth reporting of this incident: A courier's truck broke down while he was making deliveries. He called a tow truck, then persuaded the tow truck driver, pulling the courier's truck, to follow a route that just happened to coincide with the Federal Express delivery route and to stop at each delivery site! This Federal Express courier met his delivery deadline with a brokendown truck.

The policy of pushing decision-making responsibility as far down the line as possible resulted in an enlightened business decision that would *not* have been made had the courier felt constrained to follow the policy manual. (Nowhere in the Federal Express policy manual, you see, are employees given permission to make deliveries from the end of a tow truck cable.)

One authority commented upon the excellent service received at a hotel even though there was no supervisor present to influence the employee to provide that great service. He had checked in late and asked if room service was still available. The man at the desk said: "No, but if you're interested, I could go back and get a sandwich or a salad or whatever you'd like that we have in the kitchen." The man appeared to be honestly concerned about the guest's comfort and welfare.

This same traveler was impressed, again, by that hotel's employees when he observed an instance where an employee admitted a mistake to his boss when he could easily have covered it up. The traveler had ordered room service. On the way to the room, the room service person spilled the hot chocolate. It took him a few extra minutes to return to the kitchen, change the linen in the tray, and replace the drink, so he was about 15 minutes late.

The delay wasn't important to the guest. But, the next morning the room service manager phoned to apologize for the 15-minute delay and invited the guest to the buffet breakfast or a room service breakfast without charge to compensate for the inconvenience. The mistake of the employee was unknown to anyone else, but he told his manager about it, anyway.

This is what's called *service recovery*, at its best. In these situations, a service provider

Rule No. 2: If the customer is ever wrong, reread Rule No. 1.

The customer must leave satisfied.

performed above and beyond the call of duty.

To provide this level of service, you needn't believe in Dale Carnegie's rules.

No. 1: The customer is always right.

No. 2: If the customer is ever wrong, reread Rule No. 1.

But, you'd better believe in the reality spoken by John Rudeen, recent director of communication and training for SuperAmerica, a midwestern chain of convenience store/service stations. He said: "The customer is not always right, and we tell our people that from the beginning. But, customers are always customers, and we deal with them in that context."

18

*Relationships
Are Vital*

Much of our success in customer service rests upon the sense of self-esteem, trust, and confidence that we nurture in others. But, if the net result of our relationships with customers is a net loss in customers, then...

Customer relationships depend a great deal upon friendly, cooperative relations with one's boss, colleagues, and subordinates. Every person in customer service depends upon others for the assistance that they need to do their jobs well.

No matter what a person's intellectual ability or educational background, he will never achieve true success unless the peo-

Increase the odds of a promotion with a positive attitude, courtesy, respectfulness, and showing pride and professionalism on the job.

ple he works with really want to work with him. Opportunities for achievement go to those whom others like and trust.

You can *learn* to get along with others, if you want to learn badly enough. It's nice when you are born considerate and responsive. But, if you weren't, *act.* Personal development authorities such as Maxwell Maltz teach that if you pretend long enough, you begin acquiring the *pretend* trait. What the mind can conceive, the mind will believe.

In most situations you need training in customer service. That's because true customer service professionalism is rather uncommon. You can't just model your performance on the actions of other service people toward *you*, when you are a customer. If you practice what you see and experience as a customer, you are more likely to be rude and neglectful than you are to be considerate and helpful.

You will rarely learn customer service by experience, because role models are hard to find. To impress your customers with your service performance, ask yourself questions such as:

"How can I process the order sooner?"

"How can I deliver faster?"

"How can I improve my performance to support the customer?"

"How can I enhance product quality with service?"

To a large degree, if you like people in general and your customers in particular, your actions will telegraph your feelings toward them. Most customers will be appreciative and they will show their appreciation by spending more and buying often. That'll be good for you. According to one study, an employee who adopts the quality service attitude makes more money.

The words *service attitude* remind me of Hazel Brown. She began working for my companies more than 20 years ago for $2.00 an hour. Today she is Vice President of Administration, our most important executive. If anyone wanted to make a film to illustrate positive attitude, loyalty, commitment, and hard work, all they'd have to do is follow Hazel around. Her general excellence in service is obvi-

Your attitude is the chief determinant of your success.

Instead of just doing what is necessary, be concerned about the service experiences of your customers.

ous to anyone who comes in contact with her.

So, you can increase the odds of a raise or promotion with a positive attitude, courtesy, respectfulness, and showing pride and professionalism on the job. Instead of just doing what is necessary, be concerned about the service experiences of your customers and keep your commitments. You'll be known as a person who can be trusted.

19

*Doing
More Than
Necessary*

Going through the motions of providing service is one thing. Exceptional, noticeable, unusual service is quite another. You've met the people in service businesses who treat customers and clients as if they are obstacles or inconveniences instead of the source of their survival. They lounge about their work places as if they had just dropped in for a few minutes on their way to the bowling alley.

Bad service takes many forms. How many of these characters and situations do you recognize?

Going through the motions of providing service is one thing. Exceptional, noticeable, unusual service is quite another.

1) High school students working at minimum wage in a local hardware store who are so uninformed about products that any questions other than "How much does it cost?" are met with a blank stare.

2) Home electronics or computer salesmen, or auto parts store employees, who give you the feeling that you are learning-disabled because you ask questions about a product's features and applications. They toss off incomplete or unbelievable answers to questions like they would throw scraps to a dog, feeling that anyone who doesn't know *that* doesn't deserve better treatment.

3) Banks with long lines and teller windows that close just when it's your turn.

4) Doctors who are always "running late." Their office secretaries make appointments for specific times, but you haven't seen the doctor at the appointed time in ten years. Doctors apparently overschedule to maximize their incomes: Some patients might not keep their appointments, so they want another patient on site, ready to fill in at a moment's notice.

5) Salespeople who obviously feel that playing *the customer is always right* role is degrading. They give crisp, cold, and abrupt service, rarely establishing eye contact with you. They usually glance at you, just barely avoiding rudeness, because they realize that they must be helpful and friendly since that's their job, and their boss might be watching. They won't do one iota more than they must do to keep you from complaining to the manager. Service is *not* something they do with great enthusiasm.

6) In a department store, boutique, appliance store, or government office, employees walk by you as if you're a mannequin. If they can't avoid responding to you, they speak while continuing to fill in records or to stock shelves.

7) Restaurants that overbook or understaff, then encourage you to wait in the bar for your table where you buy expensive drinks.

People who earn their incomes providing service to customers whose patronage pays them should be courteous, don't you think? They should move quickly. They should be attentive, listen to customers,

Customers appreciate employees who do a good job, show that they care, and go out of their way to do a little extra.

By doing more than just enough, you will advance in your job, gain satisfaction and feel very good about yourself.

and keep their promises. They should be helpful and know enough about their product or service to answer questions.

If we consistently give poor service, some customers will exercise their option of buying elsewhere. Anybody can do just enough to get by. We can also do much more than that — more than the minimum. Customers appreciate employees who do a good job, show that they care, and go out of their way to do a little extra.

You know your job better than anyone else, if you've been doing it for a while. You can easily think of ways to improve your personal service to customers and to co-workers. With a can-do attitude, you'll be successful wherever you work and whatever you do. Your value to yourself and to everyone you come in contact with increases.

By applying yourself and doing more than just enough, you will advance farther in your job, gain more satisfaction from doing the job well, and feel very good about yourself.

You will cash in, make more money and win promotions.

Each Customer: An Individual

You will take a large step toward professionalism in your service work if you realize that each customer you deal with has different service needs and if you provide them with *customized* service.

One customer may need prompt and efficient service. Another may need recognition or assistance. Regardless of your customers needs or backgrounds, they want to be treated fairly and equally. Whatever their needs, they expect to deal with individuals who have positive attitudes and who treat them with courtesy and respect.

To meet customer expectations, treat others as you would like to be treated.

Recognize customers by name whenever possible. Greet them with a smile and make eye contact. Acknowledge customers who are waiting in line. (Sounds routine, you say? Maybe so, but how often has it happened when *you* were present?) To meet customer expectations, treat others as you would like to be treated.

View your job as value-added service. Value-added service for customers is doing anything for them that's out of the ordinary. As you go about your regular job responsibilities, look for opportunities to add value to their buying experience.

A service worker at a Cub supermarket near my home certainly added value to my buying experience. I picked up a $1.99 bag of oranges from the produce department and took it to the nearby deli department where I asked a service worker to cut the oranges into quarter sections. I was buying them for my daughter's soccer team and I only had a few minutes to get there. In about two minutes the employee was handing me a plastic bag filled with quartered oranges. This helpful employee demonstrated the reason that I spend several thousand dollars at this supermarket each year.

Take care of the need at hand first, whether it involves dealing with a customer directly or completing some other task. Then, take advantage of situations that lend themselves to doing something special.

Some people with customer service responsibilities handicap themselves by believing that customers deserve only merchandise or service that they specifically pay for. They believe that any pre-sale or post-sale service is a bonus that customers have no right to expect.

There's only one problem with this attitude. Customers believe that their money also buys polite service. When they get neglect or annoyance instead, they notice. Remember this: Quality service is whatever customers think it is.

Quality service is whatever customers think it is.

21 | *Quality*

Think about your job. If you can't find anything positive about it other than a steady pay check, you'll be doing yourself a favor by finding a new job that offers satisfying, fulfilling work.

None of us enjoy every aspect of our job. However, the positives must outweigh the negatives or we won't be very happy at all. Consider friendship, team spirit, chances for human contact, and opportunity for achievement. These are important positive factors in work that many of us overlook.

The secret to success is a job that you can commit to doing well. When we do so, we

The secret to success is a job that you can commit to doing well.

bring out the best in ourselves. Commitment is contagious. Others follow our lead.

There is an implied obligation to supervisors here. The commitment of the service pros among the people on your team must be noticed and rewarded. If it isn't, the high quality of their work may not endure.

Section

Qualities of Successful People

Victor Frankl, world-renowned philosopher who survived years in Nazi concentration camps, wrote: "Everyone has his own specific vocation or mission in life...Therein he cannot be replaced, nor can his life be repeated. Thus, everyone's task is as unique as his specific opportunity to implement it."

We *detect* rather than *invent* our missions in life, Frankl says. The mission is there, waiting for us to figure out that it is *our* mission. What he means is that each of us has an internal monitor or sense that alerts us to our uniqueness. So, trust your instincts!

"I know of no more encour- aging fact than the un- questionable ability of man to elevate his life by conscious endeavor."

Henry David Thoreau

Frankl's philosophy highlights the signifi- cance of aggressive action in our own interests. *Effective* people are opportuni- ty-minded, said Peter Drucker, famed management consultant. They *feed op- portunities* and they *starve problems*. They plot to prevent problems. *Ineffective* people live from day to day, wasting their potential.

Imagine how you would feel if you were part of a team that won the league cham- pionship when everyone expected you to win last place. Think about how you would feel if you saved a baby's life by putting your finger down her throat and pulling out a bead? Remember those times when your mind seemed white hot and you did well on some tests?

By following the suggestions in this book, you can be *white hot* regularly creative, productive, enthusiastic because you love your work. This makes you *very* effective.

You can feel inspired almost every day, if you work at it. To make it big requires enormous personal security and openness and a spirit of adventure.

22

Joy In Your Work

W. Edward Deming, the management guru who died in 1993, hammered away in his seminars at the right of all people "to have joy in their work." He estimated that no more than two in a hundred managers and ten in a hundred workers now feel happy in their work.

This is an interesting observation, considering the fact that it is difficult, indeed, to give good service unless you enjoy your work. On the other hand, people motivated by the satisfaction they derive from work become very productive and creative.

Customers like to deal with poeple who are relaxed and smiling instead of wearing a face set in plaster.

A sense of humor can put joy in your work. Reaction to humor seems to energize, thereby inducing a creative, problem-solving state of mind. Humor is *not* worthless in work.

In a report on a research project, three professors from the Hankamer School of Business at Baylor University wrote: "There is growing recognition today that something as seemingly frivolous as humor...can promote productivity and cohesion within an organization...(and) can contribute to interpersonal success and to managerial effectiveness."

""Humor expands awareness and broadens perspective...," says Dr. Harvey Mindness, an Antioch University psychologist who wrote a book entitled *Laughter and Liberation*.

So, perhaps a sense of the humorous in your work life will make you a better service provider. Customers like to deal with people who are relaxed and smiling instead of wearing a face set in plaster.

You can, however, go too far. Sometimes that which is humorous to you is just absurd to the person who was supposed to laugh. Beware.

What's more, humor helps you reduce stress. "When the going gets tough, the tough get...laughing," says Dr. Joel Goodman, director of The Humor Project at the Sagamore Institute in upstate New York. "He who laughs...lasts."

As a stress-reducing mechanism, "Humor is a tranquilizer without side effects," says Psychologist Arnold Glasow.

> *"Humor is a tranquilizer without side effects."*
> *Arnold Glasow*
> *Psychologist*

23

Humor's Benefits

Humor resolves conflict, blunts anger, prevents reckless action and calms anxiety so that you can think constructively in high-pressure situations.

Humor is a positive attitude. It makes you *want* to deliver good service. Some say that a humorous reaction to an event *reverses reality*. It *seems* to eliminate problems even though they still exist.

After all, "stress is not an event in itself, but a perception of an event," says Dr. Goodman. "People who use humor to cope with everyday problems don't show the kind of physiological responses to

Humor re-solves con-flict, blunts anger, pre-vents reckless action and calms anxiety.

stress as the humorless," he says. "It is the dead serious types who drop dead."

C.W. Metcalf, president of a company in Ft. Collins, Colorado that trains business people in the use of humor says that "the humor principle," as he calls it, is a set of skills that anyone can learn to develop. The humor principle:

- Generates enthusiasm that boosts the level of psychic energy.

- Enhances alertness and mental efficiency.

- Improves interpersonal relationships.

- Clarifies meaning and promotes understanding.

- Breaks the ice — develops cooperativeness and a feeling of camaraderie and teamwork while deflecting conflict.

- Improves concentration. Minds under stress move slowly and concentrate with difficulty.

Female employees in one Georgia company used creative humor to deflect conflict and to relieve stress. During meetings a male coworker invariably sneaked a peek under the table at the ladies' legs. He'd drop his pencil or a piece of paper or tie his shoe laces to give himself an opportunity for ogling. One day, when he pulled the same trick again, he was astounded and embarrassed to read the letters "HI, RALPH" on seven consecutive kneecaps.

The option to "HI, RALPH" that would have been chosen by some people is confrontation and anger.

A restaurant owner prevented potential controversy with humor. It seems that he couldn't stop the pilfering of his silverware. Finally, he printed this message on menus: "If you rip off one of our menus or accessories, you will automatically unlock our caged, 3,576 pound gorilla who will attack you as you leave."

Customers smiled...and abandoned any thoughts of dropping silverware into their pockets or purses.

"Learn to think funny when it's necessary to think straight."
C.W. Metcalf

"Laughter is the shortest distance between two people."

Victor Borge
Danish comic pianist

An optometrist improved relationships with his clients and put them in a cooperative mood with an office poster that read: "If you don't see what you're looking for...you're in the right place."

24 *How to Learn A Sense of Humor*

The humor strategy can be learned even by those who are certain that they are naturally somber and can't possibly learn to use humor on the job.

Goodman assures us that "humor is a learned reaction." His five techniques for learning to use humor on the job are: Practice, practice, practice, practice, and...practice.

"We're happy because we laugh, not the other way around," says Annette Goodheart, Ph.D., a psychotherapist in Santa Barbara, California. She says: "I *start* by laughing, which changes my attitudes immediately. It's easy to fake laughter."

*So, if you
want to learn
to laugh...
laugh.*

William Fry, associate clinical professor of psychiatry at Stanford University Medical School, says: "We're all born with the potential for developing a sense of humor. It's part of our genetic makeup. If most of your playful spirit has been hammered out of you by the time you reach adulthood, it can be revived."

You can keep yourself in a good mood and become prepared for life's humorous — or depressing — situations by entering jokes, anecdotes, quotes, and even bumper sticker quips in a notebook that you carry with you all the time at work. Consult the notebook when you need to find something to take the edge off of irritating, frustrating situations.

A Minneapolis man choose to react with humor instead of anger after tornado winds blew over a tree that flattened his former full-size Chevrolet into pancake thickness. He stood beside the pancake waving to passersby holding a sign that read: "COMPACT CAR."

Whenever fate presents you with an unavoidable calamity, humor can help you cope. Sometimes humor, that "reverses reality," as Dr. Goodman says, is your only constructive recourse.

Everybody has a sense of humor. Just ask them. Stephen Leacock, the famed Canadian humorist, wrote: "A man will freely confess that he has no ear for music or no taste for fiction or even no interest in religion. But, I have yet to hear a man announce that he has no sense of humor."

Remember what President John F. Kennedy said: "Three things are real God, human folly and laughter. The first two are beyond our comprehension. So we must do what we can with the third."

Why use humor? A sense of humor is one of the qualities of high achievers, says Charles Garfield, Ph.D., clinical psychologist and author of the book *Peak Performers: The New Heroes of American Business.*

> *"Humor is a learned reaction. Practice, practice, practice."*
> *Dr. Joel Goodman*

25

Empower Yourself

One way to cash in on your job is to *empower yourself.* "Take the bull by the horns," as suggested earlier.

David McNally, well-known public speaker and business consultant, was having his shoes shined. He was sitting in an elevated chair in the lobby of the Opryland Hotel in Nashville. Slap! Slap! went the shoe shine rag. The shoe shine man hummed as he worked. Quickly. Skillfully.

His name was Zee. He seemed to be about 50 years old and he loved to talk. His smile and his cheerful demeanor marked him a contented man. "I'm happy here,"

Take the bull by the horns.

said Zee. "I love what I'm doing and I make good money."

Recalling the incident, McNally said: "Not only did he treat my shoes as if they were the finest pair he'd ever seen, but his interest in me as a person had me believing I was the most fascinating individual he had ever met. Zee's enthusiasm was infectious, and he was rewarded with a line six deep waiting for his services."

McNally learned a powerful lesson from Zee, the shoe shine man who loved his job: "What we do is not as important as how and why we do it."

He believes that with a compelling reason for doing the work we do, and with attitude's such as Zee's, people are more productive and satisfied in their work. When work has meaning for workers, they *want* to be productive and creative, and they're in a mood to make friends of their customers.

Akio Morita, co-founder and chairman of Sony Corporation, said: "You encourage (employees) best not by offering more money but by offering more meaning. Though monetary compensation is important for all of us to survive, it cannot be the reason for working."

I agree; and I put this customer service spin on Morita's point: "If you don't like service work, you won't be good at it."

If you don't like service work, you won't be good at it.

Anne Pol, vice president for manufacturing operations in the mailing systems group of Pitney Bowes, says: "The key issue for people today is getting satisfaction in (their) work and feeling that (they) are making a contribution."

"It's a feeling people have always wanted," says Pol. But earlier generations were more willing to suppress desire for personal satisfaction in return for other rewards, primarily job security.

Personal happiness is more widely esteemed these days and companies have a big influence on an employee's level of happiness.

When people are recognized for the importance of their role and their contributions, they respond readily when their employers ask them to exercise creative authority and initiative in their work.

*When compa-
nies authorize
service
workers to do
whatever is
necessary,
employees
become will-
ing to take
responsibility.*

When companies authorize service workers to do whatever is necessary to make
customers happy, and when they praise
employees for their performances and
suggestions, employees become willing to
take responsibility for their own work.

Gary Boyd, manager of employee relations for the worldwide operations of
Onan Corporation, was describing empowerment when he said: "We try to
change the way people manage their
work, to change from a traditional base
to one in which we encourage people *not*
to check their brains at the door."

Forward-thinking organizations
throughout the world are beginning to
include empowerment as a critical com-
ponent of their competitive strategy.

Robert Kelley, a professor of business at
Carnegie Mellon University in Pittsburgh
and an expert on restructuring business,
says: "What we're seeing is a reawakening
of the search for meaning that character-
ized the 1960s. As baby-boomers head for
midlife, they're asking *What is it all
about?*, *What do I have to show for all my
(long) work weeks?*"

Paul J. Giddens, Manager of Human Resource Planning for General Electric Aircraft Engines in Evendale, OH, says: "I can't empower anybody. But, maybe I can get them (employees) used to the fact that they have the power *within themselves*."

You have the power within yourself.

That's what cashing in is all about. You already *have* the power. Now, *use it* if you want to make more money, get a promotion and love your job.

A love for one's work turns on the machine of empowerment that produces quality performance, creativity, and productivity. You already know that you work better when you like what you're doing.

When you feel that your work has meaning, you are more strongly motivated toward self management — toward giving people the power to act in response to a customer's need and to fully satisfy customers in the process.

Empowerment means bending or breaking the "rules" or simply just taking action to provide effective quality service to the customer's satisfaction. If the customer wins, you win. For empowerment to work

*Empower-
ment means
bending or
breaking the
"rules" or
simply just
taking action
to provide
effective
quality
service to the
customer's
satisfaction.*

you have to take the initiative to take care of the customer to their satisfaction, not your satisfaction or your company's satisfaction. The emotional impact on the customer is far more meaningful if you take action on your own without waiting for someone else's approval.

Sometimes it's easier to ask for forgiveness after you take action. Your goal is to be the best service professional in your industry. This helps your organization and the customer.

But, *taking* more power than your employer is *giving* can be dangerous. If you entertain thoughts of retiring with a pension from your present employment, you would be wise to get your boss's approval to act in response to a customer's needs, as you see them. Be aware that many managers are not enthusiastic about empowerment. They feel that it takes away some of their power. They like being *bosses* instead of only *coaches*. Their problem is that they don't know how to delegate responsibility without feeling less important.

Here's where you come in. If you want to cash in at your job, practice a little careful leadership. Try to influence your manager and your fellow employees to see the value for the customer of more empowerment for the people (you and your peers) who actually deal with employees face to face and ear to ear.

The benefits of empowerment will not be seen in a company without middle and senior managers who are *committed* to it. Some executives ridicule empowerment because they think that it makes it easier for customers to take advantage of them.

On the other hand, some employees resist empowerment because they're afraid of the anger of their supervisors or of other consequences of making a bad empowered decision.

If they are to be creative and productive, workers *must* be empowered. They must be given permission to manage themselves and to think for themselves. They must be allowed to evaluate themselves and to make adjustments.

Irritable exchanges between customers and clerks sometimes result when company policy withholds authority from clerks.

If you are to be creative and productive, you must be empowered.

*Empower-
ment means
clearly
defining that
customers
come first.*

"The customer goes crazy when he asks if he can return a $5 item and the answer is *I don't know, I have to ask my manager*," says Harry Thompson, a distributor of training films. "An employee who feels reduced to a dumbo is likely to project that to a customer."

Fidelity Bank of Philadelphia increased customer service representatives' wages by 58 percent over two years while authorizing them to resolve all customer problems involving less than $1,000. Customer satisfaction, as measured by their willingness to recommend the bank to a friend, jumped from 65 percent to 90 percent. This loyalty translates into increased profits. At the same time, total cost of resolving small-scale customer problems actually declined due to the elimination of time-consuming bureaucratic steps.

Empowerment means clearly defining that customers come first — encouraging people to act to meet customer needs, allowing employees to make mistakes, training all employees in the skills and techniques of quality service.

To expedite empowerment, managers need to :

1) Listen to employees.

2) Not critique employees who take empowered action.

3) Reinforce and reward employees when they take empowered action.

4) Treat people as partners who own their jobs.

5) Respect people's interests and accept different styles and methods.

6) Make performance, not credentials, the most important basis for employee evaluation.

What you do is not as important as how and why you do it.

Time

If you're going to cash in, in this service society, you need to learn how to make the best possible use of your time.

The first step in optimizing your time is to set priorities. The essence of the best thinking in time management is captured in a single phrase: Organize — and execute around priorities. When you prioritize, you think ahead. You work on the roots of problems. You work on activities that *prevent* problems so that there will be fewer problems to *solve*. (You'll never eliminate *all* problems before they occur.)

Learn how to make the best possible use of your time.

Remember that when you prioritize you are making *efficient* use of your time. You are applying the Pareto Principle: 80 percent of the results of one's labors flow out of 20 percent of the activities.

Famed Management Consultant Peter F. Drucker says that you shouldn't schedule work deadlines. Instead, devise ways to use your time efficiently. "If you plan *work*, your plan usually remains just a collection of good intentions." It *is* alright to write down your objectives clearly. Writing crystallizes thought and crystallized thought motivates action.

Here are some inside tips on becoming personally service driven:

- Plan efficient use of time. Make a point of doing the most important or difficult things first.

- Make small decisions promptly.

- In most matters any decision is better than no decision.

- Exceed customer expectations and consistently fill customer requests one day ahead of schedule.

- List major goals for both the short term (six months) and long term (more than a year). Then list activities that will carry you toward these goals.

- Group related and similar activities and do them at the same time. Doing so saves time and effort.

- Act now. Do not procrastinate. The basic reason for putting off action usually is just plain fear.

Drucker also suggests keeping a time log to identify gaps in your schedule. When you know where the gaps are, then you are equipped to plug the gaps. (There's no rule stating that only bosses can keep time logs.)

Some people keep a continuous log and examine it every month. Others keep a log for three or four weeks every six months. After each period they reappraise and re-work their schedules.

A final tip: Accept responsibility for *allowing* others to waste your time. It is as much your response to their actions as it is to the actions themselves that waste time.

Don't kill time
— It has no
ressurection.

You will give your career a boost when you work hard at time management.

For instance, if you listen to long, one-way conversations with a patient look on your face until the person is finished, you will find that politeness consumes your days — and produces disgruntled customers waiting for you to finish.

Instead of enduring the destruction of your time, learn how to interrupt politely.

You will give your career a boost when you work hard at time management. Knowing how to get the most possible quality production out of your time can do a lot to make you successful.

27

Service Recovery

Whether we realize it or not, most human behavior consists of problem solving. Dealing with problems isn't peripheral to life. Problem solving is the essence of life — the way successful lives are lived.

Great customer service professionals are quick on their feet. When a customer turns blue with rage, they still manage to send them away smiling.

When a customer is told that her sewing machine hasn't been repaired by the promised time, the customer departs saying under her breath: "These guys are idiots."

Service recovery is doing something extra for the customer at no charge after you screw up.

Service recovery is doing something extra for the customer at no charge after you or your organization screw up. This must be something that has *value* in the customer's eyes.

Think. What is it that you can do for a customer or give to them that motivates them to say: "Wow!" or "These guys are *good!*"

All of us make mistakes. Out responses to these mistakes — service recovery — separates the pros from the amateurs in customer service.

My son received cold French fries at a McDonald's fast food restaurant. He brought the fries back into the store and the employee apologized and gave him three or four times the portion of fries that he paid for...and they were *hot*.

Perhaps those fries cost McDonald's a nickel. But, the empowered employee's action might have earned the company hundreds of dollars in purchases by my son who now seems to worship McDonald's.

Say that a restaurant took a long time to seat you. The hostess apologizes and offers you a free round of drinks. The cost? Peanuts. The benefit? Loyal customers.

All of us have something we can do or give away that doesn't cost a fortune. We need to delight or *wow* the customer. Service recovery builds customer loyalty and helps you keep customers.

If you are determined to practice service recovery (solving service problems to the satisfaction of customers), then get rid of useless emotions such as guilt and worry. Guilt shackles you to the past and worry projects you into an imagined future that's almost always worse than it turns out to be.

As psychologist Wayne Dyer notes, neither guilt nor worry change anything. They only rob you of the confidence and self esteem that you need to tackle problems. By indulging in the luxury of emotion, you are distracted from the problem. Energy, that should be used to solve a problem, is being burned off.

Fault-finding and blaming undermine your ability to deal with the problems

Service recovery builds customer loyalty and helps you keep customers.

Fault-finding and blaming undermine your ability to deal with problems.

presented by customers who expect the impossible. When you spend time and energy cursing fate or railing against people or circumstances, you are simply expressing frustration. You are not correcting the problem.

By blaming, you persuade yourself that you are a victim and that you are not capable of righting what's wrong. That attitude is a powerful handicap.

True service professionals don't go overboard in their effort to prove that an irate customer is wrong and *they* are right. They concentrate instead upon gathering enough information to solve the problem.

They get the customer to focus on the specific complaint that's at the root of a general complaint.

They avoid use of the pronoun "you" or language implying that the customer caused the problem. The most common example — "You failed to enclosed payment" — leaves no room for the possibility that the check was lost, misposted, or stolen and places unnecessary blame on the customer. The object is to get the check, not to assign responsibility.

You can neutralize such a statement by saying: "The check appears to have been omitted. Has it turned up there?" This no-fault approach suggests that an abstract third party (not "you") simply may have forgotten to enclose the check.

Another useful neutral approach is to call an error to the customer's attention through rephrasing and paraphrasing: "Let me see if I have this right..."

Often, the customer will immediately see the error without prompting, by virtue of having heard it phrased differently by another person without using judgmental language.

Service professionals don't argue with the facts or try to persuade a customer that the buyer is wrong and the seller is right. They listen. They respond. They seek out customer comments and take them to heart.

Those who are the most successful at understanding and solving problems — at practicing service recovery — seem to have both self confidence and esteem for customers. Let that be a lesson.

Service professionals don't argue with the facts or try to prove a customer wrong.

28

Energize

If you're going to succeed in a service society, you'll need energy. Lots of it. Energy is a pre-requisite of motivation. Obviously, a person who's always tired isn't going to be highly motivated.

It's assumed that you'll get enough sleep. The amount of sleep that you need, say experts, varies between 6 and 10 hours, or so. Most people are refreshed after 6 to 8 hours. You'll get more done in less time if your body is rested.

Eat well and regularly. Lay off the sweets they give you a quick but short boost *always* followed by a period of low energy. Learn your coffee limit. To exceed

Understand who you are and what you are capable of.

the limit is to *reduce* your energy, not to increase it.

Have some fun during your non-work hours. For high motivation a human being needs a life balanced between work *and* play, say psychologists.

It's a surprise to some people that there's as much energy in the emotional aspects of life as in the physical aspects. Certainly, good health energizes and motivates, but so does an accepting self-image.

To like yourself is better than self-criticism. Liking yourself doesn't require conceit. It's not conceited to accept yourself as being as worthy as anyone else.

Develop a healthy self-image. Understand who you are and what you are capable of accomplishing. When you do, life is less threatening.

Don't constantly try to convince others that you are a worthwhile person. It's not necessary that you are universally loved when you know inside that you are a decent person.

It's important to have friends who like themselves, too. Friends with low self esteem tend to knock down your own self esteem. Most of us have enough trouble keeping our psyches pumped up without enduring the handicap of other people's low self-esteem.

Another emotional source of energy is a concept of yourself as a unique individual. No one else on earth is exactly like you. Avoid constantly comparing yourself and your performance with the performance of co-workers. The only meaningful comparison, for you, is between what you are *now* and what you can *become*.

Remove the limitations that you impose upon yourself. The familiar nine-dot exercise is an example. The instructions are to connect all nine dots with four straight lines without lifting your pen from the paper. The only thing that will prevent you from doing so is your own self imposed limitation.

Most people cannot follow the instructions to successfully complete the exercise because they force themselves to end each line at a dot. The trick is to extend two of the lines *beyond* the edge dots. (You will

Stop thinking about what others are doing or where they are.

Today is the first day of the rest and the best of your life.

find the correct way of connecting the dots at the end of the book.)

In that way, every day is a chance for a new beginning. Today is the first day of the *rest* and the *best* of your life. You can *still* become a big success.

29

Leisure

All of us *need* fulfilling leisure activity —activity that appeals to each of us, personally. This fulfilling activity *recharges* our psychic batteries and restores enthusiasm for work. Without fun in life we're likely to find boredom. Boredom is a dead battery, a walking coma. Any activity seems difficult or too much trouble. Arising from a sofa and walking to the front door requires dogged willpower for one who is *bored*.

"The bored often are called lazy," observes Dr. Richard Barthol, an associate professor of psychology at the University of California at Los Angeles. "When one is

Boredom is a dead battery, a walking coma.

bored, bodily functions slow down and you feel sluggish," he says.

Boredom can be diminished by leisure-time fun. For people who work full-time, most fun time is relegated to weekends or to other days off. That puts a lot of pressure on weekends.

Without weekend fun, some people contract "Monday Fever," reports Rome's Institute of Labor Medicine. Its flu-like symptoms are headache, sleepiness, fever and breathlessness.

A study found that more heart attacks occur at work on Monday than on any other day of the week.

The University of Manitoba in Winnipeg, Canada studied 4,000 men for 32 years. They found that 63 of them died suddenly, though their medical history showed no previous heart problems. Of those men, 22 died on Mondays — more than three times any other day but Thursday when 13 died.

In the *Journal of the American Medical Association* researchers hypothesized the cause of the Monday heart attacks, perhaps the cause of Monday Fever, too: "Reintroduction to occupational stress, activity, or pollutants after a weekend respite may be factors precipitating the arrhythmias that are the presumed bases for sudden death."

Weekends or days off are very important to people who work all week. Unfortunately, for many people days off are spent *couch potatoing*. They sleep late Saturday and Sunday morning. The rest of the weekend they do nothing, explaining to themselves that they *deserve* the dormancy after working hard all week.

Dr. Bruce Morehouse, Ph.D., proprietor of The Leisure Company of Santa Monica, Califonia, thinks that people need some *structure* on days off. For many years they've been conditioned to function according to schedules in school, perhaps in the military, during their early work years, and so on.

If they leave themselves without a plan, direction, and at least a loose schedule on days off they are likely to lapse into passivity.

Without at least a loose schedule on days off, you are likely to lapse into passivity.

30

*Weekend
Neurosis*

Says Steven A. Shapiro, MD, a psychotherapist: "Without a schedule
and assignments people who work all
week often face a whole string of anxieties
on weekends. Weekend Neurosis victims
feel irritable, depressed and restless. By
the end of the weekend they may suffer
abdominal pains and headaches."

(Headaches? A study at the Center Ce-
falee dell 'Universita in Torino, Italy,
found that 46 of 104 subjects in a study
experienced headaches *only* on weekends.)

To avoid weekend neurosis (even if your
weekend is not on Saturday and Sunday),

"Enthusiasm is important because work done enthusiastically is work done well."

Sam Keen
Psychologist

and to have real fun, find leisure that's right for *you*. Beware of knee-jerk leisure, fun chosen because it's favored by friends and relatives or a leisure activity pursued simply because it's been done for years, it's convenient, or it's in vogue. This kind of fun is likely to be *funless* fun. Participants go through the motions of having fun without feeling pleasure.

The desirable alternative is leisure activity customized to one's basic nature.

Real fun revives the over-worked and the over-stressed by stimulating their spirits, restoring enthusiasm...and easing stress.

"Fun revives enthusiasm," says psychologist Sam Keen who wrote *What To Do When You're Bored and Blue*. "Enthusiasm is important because work done enthusiastically is work done well," he says.

In the early 20th century it was not common for people to make *work* out of their leisure activity, as they do today. Today, "He works hard and he plays hard" is a compliment.

Skilled play and self-improvement recreation are favored by many. Aggressive, highly-competitive play is honored. And *fast fun* that allows prompt return to work has achieved popularity.

Much leisure has become "contaminated leisure," says Harry Levinson, lecturer in the department of psychiatry at Harvard Medical School. People golf or fish so intensely that they derive no sense of relief or pleasure from the recreation.

What a person needs, instead, is quality recreation — activity fit for *you* and done just for the fun of it. The primary definition of recreation in the *Oxford English Dictionary* is "Time which one spends as one pleases." The activity itself (the process) should be valued more highly than any product of the activity such as ego satisfaction derived from winning.

A fisherman who enjoys the ambience of the lake is likely to have more fun than a determined, jut-jawed fisherman who has *got* to catch his limit of fish or grumble all the way home and vow to never fish again. Fish because you love the peace of an afternoon under the sun on a lake. Don't feel that you absolutely must catch fish or you'll be embarrassed when

You need quality recreation — activity fit for you and done just for the fun of it.

"Hapiness depends on leisure."

Aristotle

family and friends discover your empty creel.

Let "weekend" be a word with the instant impact of "Christmas Eve," "raise in pay," or "new car."

One man has a reputation in his community for his green thumb. His vegetable garden with its stands of sweet corn and plots of tomatoes and green beans supply all his nearby neighbors and relatives most of the summer. That's a good example of leisure activity chosen because the *participant* enjoyed it.

"It is commonly believed that happiness depends on leisure," Aristotle wrote in his *Ethics*, "because we occupy ourselves so that we may have leisure, just as we make war in order that we may live at peace."

Conclusion

The one trait more than any other that marks a winner is the fact that a winner *never* quits.

You *can* be a winner. Fix that objective in your mind, work like a migrant laborer in the vegetable fields, and *never* give up.

"Never give in...never, never, never...in nothing, great or small, large or petty never give in except to convictions of honor or good taste," said Winston Churchill as the inspirational Prime Minister of England during World War II.

There are no *reasons* that you cannot succeed. There are only *handicaps*. They

"Never give in...never, never, never... in nothing, great or small, large or petty..."
Winston Churchill

are reasons why success might be delayed. Just delayed, not cancelled.

You have freedom of choice. You can *choose* to work hard to achieve goals. You can also *choose* to sacrifice money, time, convenience to be successful.

Some people may have been muddling along for years, wondering why they haven't succeeded. People such as this often benefit from *unlearning* the attitudes and practices that have been ineffective for them, thereby creating intellectual space for new learning. By doing so they create room for new attitudes and practices.

The personal philosophy of Bruce Lee, the famous martial artist, was that a learner's glass must be *empty* if he is to learn. If, instead, his glass is full of existing facts, beliefs, and attitudes, then the learner has some unlearning to do.

Bruce Lee told the story of a Japanese Zen master who was visited by an American university professor. The professor asked for knowledge, though he attempted to impress the martial arts master with the high level of his existing knowledge of the martial arts.

The master did not respond to the request. Instead, he asked the college professor to have tea with him. Instructing him to watch, the master poured the tea. He continued to pour after the tea began to flow over the edge of the cup and to run in rivulets to the edge of the table and down onto the floor.

Startled, the American professor asked: "Why did you do that?"

Martial Arts Master: "When a man's cup is overflowing he cannot learn. He learns only when his cup is not full and he is *ready* to have it filled."

Do you want to have a full cup? Do you want to "cash in" and make more money?

If you do, beware of these mistakes:

(1) Negative Habit Patterns: Associate primarily with people who think and live positively, who expect success to emerge from any weed patch. Read everything with a positive slant that you can find to feed your mind with positive ideas.

Listen to personal development and self-improvement recordings. You can find

There is no reason that you cannot succeed.

View mistakes as an opportunity for growth.

such material at any library or bookstore.

Beware of negative thinking. Positive thinking is very important because the key to personal growth is your confidence in your ability to change yourself and your attitudes.

(2) Reliving Past Failures: Mistakes are neither black marks on your record nor indications of weakness. They are important parts of the learning process. View mistakes as an inevitable part of life, an opportunity for growth, and a maturing experience.

A healthy-minded person can enjoy analyzing a mistake and milking it of all its potential lessons. A mistake then becomes a victory and a once-in-a-lifetime opportunity.

This is not pointless rationalization. It is a constructive, goal-directed interpretation of reality that allows you to face all of life realistically and without fear, instead of denying reality or hiding from life's inevitable events.

If you intend to cash in on your career, you are determined to work as hard as you must to make it, you are certain that mistakes are just learning events, and if you have learned the strategies and tactics of success seeking, then you *will* succeed.

Don't worry about it. Just keep working. And learning.

If you intend to cash in on your career, then you will succeed.

Management: Support Employee Education

Begin a campaign to persuade management to help you and others in your personal development quest. Show this section to your supervisor.

You've heard it said: "This is a service society."

We've reached the point in this service society where consumers *expect* good service. They quickly notice the bad service that differentiates one company from a competitor.

It is your front-line service providers and those who equip them to provide good

This is a service society.

service (behind-the-scenes employees) who *deliver* the services...that *create* the impressions...that *build* the reputation...that *pays off* in repeat sales, in more sales, and in customer satisfaction and referrals.

When customers think about your company, the images that flash in their minds are the faces of employees they deal with. They aren't visualizing your vice presidents when they think about and talk about Wal-Mart or Federal Express.

Service providers are the most important impression-creating element of your company. Sales prices, location, products, and services attract customers one time, but it is the quality of the service provided by service providers that brings customers back a second time...and a third and fourth time.

By being helpful and supportive and by showing courtesy and respect, employees deliver quality customer service and customers gladly return to buy from you again.

The human resources of a company have unique value among all your resources:

Only *people* think. As a result, management of service providers requires the supreme attention of company executives.

The success or failure of corporate strategy lies in the human resources policy. Yet, companies spend most of their training dollars on supervisors and managers. Money is also spent on training new hires on product knowledge and technical training.

What we have is a systematic undervaluation of the importance of employees. Underestimation of the value of human resources becomes a self-fulfilling prophecy. It translates into training that turns out badly-educated workers with narrow skills that quickly become outdated and unnecessary.

Untrained or poorly trained employees are *expensive*. They tend to leave sooner than well-trained employees. This makes it necessary for you to spend money to find replacements and to prepare them for their new jobs.

Service providers trained in the means of delivering customer service remain on the

It is the quality of the service provided that brings customers back.

Untrained or poorly trained employees are expensive.

job longer largely because they derive greater satisfaction from their work. We find many service and retail organizations that talk a lot about satisfying customers, but they almost entirely neglect the people who do the job of satisfying them the employees.

To be successful in a service society, companies must, of course, provide service. They must facilitate the service activities of service providers.

The spirit of service that arises from basic personal feelings about self, work, and other people must come alive, stay alive, grow, and flourish if an organization is to leap beyond the bounds of mediocrity.

That spirit blooms when employees are *empowered* with the decision-making authority to do whatever needs to be done to achieve customer satisfaction.

To empower employees, companies must *educate* employees. At the least, they must help employees educate themselves.

Empower experienced professionals to get the job done and to be resourceful and creative in doing so, without requiring management approval for any action that was not grandfathered in from the Nixon presidency. Then make sure that managers provide the environment, help, and tools that service providers need.

Many admirable customer service intentions were sabotaged by failure to supply employees with the training and the tools that were indispensable in providing the intended service.

Empowered, self-managed employees become *self-motivated*.

Training all employees regularly would severely strain the capacity of some independent and smaller companies to continue in business. That's why it's a very smart move to do everything you can afford to do in *helping* service professionals reach for the brass ring on their own time.

You can't *buy* a person's enthusiasm and the eager application of his or her brainpower. All your compensation buys is a person's presence and, usually, the performance of certain overt tasks. To win an employee's loyalty, creativity, ingenu-

You can't buy a person's enthusiasm and the eager application of brainpower.

To win an employee's loyalty, creativity, ingenuity, and resourcefulness, you must earn and inspire them.

ity, and resourcefulness you must *earn* and *inspire* them.

Trained service providers are important to the success of your business. Research shows that people trained formally in the workplace have a 30 percent higher productivity rate after one year than people who are not formally trained. (Bishop, 1989)

Think of employees as volunteers. They *volunteer* their enthusiasm, good will, and creative minds. It is employers who have the responsibility to arouse that enthusiasm in the first place.

Developing an employee's pride in their job, in themselves, and in their employer is an effective way to earn and inspire an employee's heart and mind — to convert them into volunteers.

The Coleman Company of Wichita, Kansas develops employee pride with its *Outstanding Employee* performance recognition programs. Articles in the company newsletter report outstanding customer service performance. Coleman is the world's largest manufacturer of camping and outdoor recreation equipment.

Recognition programs are one of a thousand ways to develop the pride that generates enthusiasm, essential to quality customer service performance.

Empowerment + motivation + knowledge = Resourcefulness. Personal resourcefulness is extrememly useful in a service economy.

Empower employees to increase their own knowledge. That's a motivating combination. To do so you can:

- Loan equipment such as video players for service providers to use at home or after hours at work. Let them check out tapes, films, and videos.

- Publish informative articles in the company newsletter or magazine. Distribute literature obtained from industry sources.

- Allow employees to attend seminars with pay.

Empower-ment
+ motivation
+ knowledge
= Resource-fulness

The mere awareness that the company is behind self-development of employees is motivational for them.

The mere awareness that the company is behind self-development of employees is motivational for them. To establish a clear company commitment to employee self-development in customer service, write and publish:

Vision Statement: An image of what management wants the organization to become. It is the desired future state for the business, particularly as it relates to customer value and service quality.

Mission Statement: A simple, compelling description of how the organization wants to do business, in terms of customers and customer value.

Core Values Statement: Critical values to which the people in the organization must commit their energies. Core values are those essential to accomplishing the mission and achieving the vision.

Such a plan focuses employee self development. One more thing you can do: Give each employee a copy of this book.

Most people cannot follow the instructions to successfully complete the exercise because they force themselves to end each line at a dot. The trick is to extend two of the lines beyond the edge dots. (The exercise can be found on page 160.)

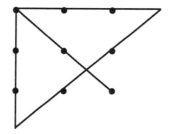